THE OFFICIAL FROME TOWN FOOTBALL CLUB QUIZ BOOK

600 QUESTIONS COVERING
THE CLUB'S HISTORY

Including memoirs of The Hill

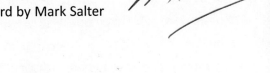

To PATRICK,
UP THE ROBINS!
BEST WISHES

Compiled by Kevin Snelgrove
Foreword by Mark Salter

Apex Publishing Ltd

PUBLISHER INFORMATION

First published as an eBook and Paperback in 2019 by

Apex Publishing Ltd

307 Holland Road, Holland on Sea, Essex, CO15 6PD, United Kingdom

www.apexpublishing.co.uk

* Please email any queries to: mail@apexpublishing.co.uk

Copyright © 2019 Kevin Snelgrove

The author has asserted his moral rights

ISBN: 978-1-911476-62-7

Cover design: Hannah Blamires

Cover Pictures courtesy of Steve McCarthy www.stevemccarthy-photography.co.uk Justin Paget, Nicholas Peet and Frome Town Football Club

This book is an official product of Frome Town Football Club

Dedicated to all players, managers and staff involved in
FROME TOWN FOOTBALL CLUB
Since the club's formation

In memory of
Paul Antony Snelgrove (1962-2000)
Bill (1934-2010) & Brenda (1936-2017) Harding
Dawn Prior (1960-2018)

ACKNOWLEDGEMENTS

A special thank you to:
Mark Salter for writing the Foreword
Jeremy Alderman – Chairman
Gary Collinson - Football & Operations Director
Simon Harding – Club Shop Manager
Shaun 'Basher' Baker - Kit Manager
Sally Lacey – Programme & Refreshment Sales
Colin Carpenter - Match Reporter
Ivan Carver – Vice Chairman
Scott Fitzgibbon – Marketing & Commercial Manager
Geoff Morton-Norris – Chairman of the Supporters Club
Justin Paget – Frome Town FC Women Manager
Ian Pearce – Former Frome Town FC Secretary & Statistician
Kerry Miller - *'The Boys on the Hill'* - *The Official History of Frome Town FC* (2011)
Chris Cowlin – Publishing Manager of Apex Publishing Limited

Paul Antell, Terry Atkinson, Trevor Atkinson, Luke Ballinger, Ryan Bath, Paul Bendell, James Billing, Aaron Blacker, Mary Brant, Mae Bristow, Alison Bryant, John Bryant, Nick Bunyard, Jon Burr, Jamie Cheeseman, Darren Chitty, Enna-Marie Christmas, Matty Cowler, Jon Crowley, Rick Davis, Laura Didymus, Karl Diment, Colin Dredge, Mandy Dredge, Sam Duggan, Nieve Edwards, Grant Evason, Paul Farrell, Richard Fey, Sapphire Fitzgibbon, Joe Gomes, Johnny Gorman, Derek Graham, Theresa Graham, Danny Greaves, Dean Griffiths, Maisie Harris, Simon Hillman, Shane Hobbs, Ricky Hulbert, Steph Isaacson, Josh Jeffries, Simon Keates, Ollie Knowles, Alex Lapham, Lisa Lewer, Gary Lewis, Jon McAlinden, Jack Metcalf, Kris Miller, Jamie Mines, Adamo Missiato, Alex Monks, Justin Paget, Nicholas Peet, Karen Perkins, Andrew Perrett, Darren Perrin, Matthew Peters, Emily Petteford, Zoe Porch, Dean Ranger, Paul Randall, Charley Ratcliffe, Steve Ratcliffe, Joe Raynes, Betty Restorick, Connor Roberts, Maya Seviour, Dave Smith, John Southern, Giuseppe Sorbara, Sam Teale, Ben Thomson, Paul Thorpe, Keira-Leigh Underhill, Tim Vine and Asa Wilkinson for their memories and endorsements.

FOREWORD

It is a real privilege to be asked by Kevin Snelgrove to write the foreword to this book and be given the opportunity to look back on the fantastic memories I have as a player for Frome Town FC. I am exceptionally grateful to everyone, who not only helped me as a player but have also had a huge influence on the club and its success over the years.

I can remember as a nineteen-year old being given the chance by Kingsley John to join him at Frome Town and make the step up to Western League Football. When I arrived for my first training session back in July 1999, I could immediately see that the new Chairman Paul McGuiness was starting to make changes at Badgers Hill. A new stand was being erected and the bar area was being spruced up ready for the following season. The pitch however looked like it was in desperate need of some water, with the length of the brown grass more like a hay field, which is a far cry from the football pitch I enjoyed playing on for so many seasons and that we see today.

I made my debut on 14th August 1999 after making the long trip down to Ilfracombe. A ground, for those that know it, where you play up hill in both the first and second half. Despite a 3-1 defeat, I did manage to score my first goal for the club. However, that first season was a challenging one, finishing at the bottom of the first division, although somehow avoiding relegation. I spent most of the season playing at right back but ended the season as top goal scorer with 12 goals.

Within a couple of years and under the management of Simon White we had one of the most memorable and successful seasons, winning the first division in style accumulating 102 points and reaching the Les Philips cup final at Twerton Park. I remember vividly the huge array of flags draped over the terraces behind the goal and the large following of supporters singing until the final whistle!

After a brief time away with Southend United and Bath City, Paul McGuiness made it possible for me to return to the club. I had an amazing 7 years, with some of the highlights being a goal tally of 46 in the 2006/07 season, captaining the side which went on to win the Somerset Premier Cup and getting promotion to the Southern League. I was also fortunate enough to play in the team that reached the quarter finals of the FA Vase, finally losing out to Jarrow Roofing.

I am extremely grateful to everyone who was involved with the club and I was privileged to have played for some great managers over the years. I still bump in to a few of them with the likes of Andy Black, Paul Thorpe and Andy Crabtree, who are still involved with local clubs. I also had the pleasure of playing with some excellent players, getting to know some great people and establishing some really good friendships whilst playing for Frome.

Frome Town is a very special club with fantastic people and wonderful support. I think that most players that have been fortunate enough to play for the club will have fond memories of their time at Frome Town.

The club has been a big part of my life and my family's, particularly my Dad 'John' and I feel honoured to have contributed to the club's history with a total of 450 appearances and 292 goals.

I always check Frome Town's results every Saturday and hope that the football club continues to be successful and there are more trophies to come.

Best Wishes

Mark Salter
1999-2002 & 2003-10

INTRODUCTION

I would first like to thank all the staff at Frome Town Football Club for their help on this project. I have been a fan of this wonderful club since 1978 and have seen many highs and lows during this time. I can remember watching many home games stood at the Club house end with my late brother Paul and later-on with my daughters Samantha and Kate they were enjoyable days. With the likes of Dave Allen and Mark Salter scoring many goals, and the ever-present Steve Walkey and Centre-half Paul Thorpe all club legends along with many more who have worn the Frome shirt.

These days I don't seem to get so much time as I would like attending the games but still keep up with the results and I have recently been watching the Frome Town Women on a Sunday and what a great team they have and I've been very impressed.

I hope you enjoy this book. Hopefully it should bring back some wonderful memories!

I have provided you with some very easy and very hard questions, so there is a good mixture.

In closing, I would like to thank all my friends and family for encouraging me to complete this book.

Best Wishes

Kevin Snelgrove

www.apexpublishing.co.uk

QUESTIONS

CLUB HISTORY

1. Which year was Frome Town Football Club founded?

2. What is Frome Town's nickname?

3. Which season did Frome Town join the Western League playing in Division Two?

4. Which ground do Frome Town play their home matches?

5. What is the capacity of Frome Town's stadium – 1,331, 2,331 or 3,331?

6. Which year did Frome Town add a 250-seater east stand so their ground would meet the requirements set out for the Southern Football League Premier Division?

7. Which team did Frome Town beat 3-1 to win the Somerset Premier Cup in 2008/09?

8. Who was made Frome Town's manager for the 2018/19 season?

9. In 1911/12 season Frome Town reached the fifth qualifying round of the FA Cup losing away to Southport Central in front of 3,366 but what was the score – 2-1, 4-1 or 6-1?

10. What was Frome Town's nickname before the Great War?

CLUB RECORDS

11. How many appearances did Mark Salter make in his Frome Town career?

12. What position did Frome Town finish in the Southern League Premier Division of 2016/17?

13. What is Frome Town's highest home attendance, which was vs. Leyton Orient in the 1st Round of the FA Cup in 1954/55?

14. Which club defeated Frome Town 4-0 away in the second round of the FA Trophy in 1984-85 season?

15. True or false: Frome Town reached the quarter-final of the FA Vase in 2004/05 before being beaten by Jarrow Roofing 3-0?

16. Which year did Frome Town win the FA Community Club of the Year (Somerset)?

17. Which year was Frome Town promoted to the Southern League Premier Division for the first time?

18. In the 1930s and 1940s which player scored 212 goals in 260 appearances for Frome Town?

19. Which player in the 1970s and 1980s scored over 260 goals for Frome Town first team and the reserves combined?

20. Who is Frome Town's all-time leading goal scorer in all competitions with 292 goals?

CLUB HONOURS

Match the season with the Frome Town honour

21. Western League Premier Division Winners

22. Wiltshire Football League Premier Division Winners

23. Somerset Premier Cup Winners

24. Western Football League Cup Winners

25. Western League Division Two Runners-up

26. Southern Football League Cup Runners-up

27. Somerset Senior Cup Winners

28. Western League Division One Winners

29. Somerset County Football League Premier Division Winners

30. Western Counties Floodlit Cup Winners

1906/07, 1909/10, 1932/33, 1954/55, 1966/67, 1978/79, 1982/83, 1983/84, 2001/02, 2012/13.

WHERE DID THEY COME FROM? -1

*Match the player with the club they joined
Frome Town FC from?*

31. Tony Pounder

32. Richard Fey

33. Steve Book (first spell)

34. Paul Randall

35. Brian Drysdale

36. Phil Purnell

37. Wyndham Haines

38. Ronnie Briggs

39. Mark Salter (second spell)

40. Bryan Wade

Bath City, Brighton & Hove Albion, Bristol Manor Farm, Bristol Rovers, Forest Green Rovers, Glastonbury Town, Oxford United, Paulton Rovers, Weymouth Town, Yeovil Town.

LEGENDS – 1

Re-arrange the letters to reveal the Frome Town FC legend

41.   ORY TABLETTR

42.   SELLIE ROYLAT

43.   NOHJ TAGTGEM

44.   ODGU YARDWAH

45.   AVED NALLE

46.   DOR SAMAD

47.   EVETS KEYLAW

48.   KARM TREALS

49.   LAPU ROPETH

50.   TEVES YAG

POSITIONS IN THE LEAGUE – 1

Match the season with the position Frome Town FC finished

51.   2017/18 Southern League Premier Division, 61 points

52.   1975/76 Western League, 61 points

53.   1983/84 Western League Premier Division, 50 points

54.   1919/20 Western League Division Two, 22 points

55.   1989/90 Western League Premier Division, 26 points

56.   2008/09 Western League Premier Division, 76 points

57.   1955/56 Western League Division One, 27 points

58.   1931/32 Western League Division Two, 37 points

59.   1998/99 Western League Division One, 26 points

60.   2005/06 Western League Premier Division, 64 points

1st, 2nd, 4th, 7th, 8th, 10th, 11th, 13th, 17th, 20th.

RANDOM SELECTION – 1

61. Which band sings the 1982 song "A Town Called Malice" when Frome Town make their entrance at home games?

62. Which team did Frome Town defeat 4-1 in their first ever competitive game at Badgers Hill on 3rd September 1904 in the Wiltshire League?

63. After a poor start to the 2003/04 season Frome Town struggled to win at home so they turned for help from a local "White Witch" what was her name?

64. What are the measurements of Frome Town's pitch – 104 x 65m, 106 x 67m or 108 x 69m?

65. What colour is Frome Town's away kit for 2018/19 season?

66. Which Frome Hotel was Frome Town FC formed in on 7 June 1904?

67. Which Frome Town player was voted club 'Sportsman of the Year' in 1962?

68. How many first team goals did Steve Gay score in his Frome Town career – 71, 81 or 91?

69. How many first team goals was score by Frome Town in the 1947/48 season - 100, 107 or 114?

70. How many points did Frome Town end the 2001/02 season with from 38 games played – 100, 102 or 104?

AWAY DAYS – 1

If Frome Town would be playing at the following grounds, which team would they be playing against?

71.   The Bob Lucas Stadium

72.   Penydarren Park

73.   The Camrose

74.   The Memorial Fields

75.   The Rushmoor Stadium

76.   Earlsmead Stadium

77.   The Avenue Stadium

78.   Wheatsheaf Park

79.   Holloways Park

80.   The Cuthbury

THROUGH THE DECADES - 1

Can you match the average League wins per season Frome Town had with the decade?

81.   1904-20 (Five seasons less because of World War 1)

82.   1921-30

83.   1931-40

84.   1945-50 (Five seasons less because of World War2)

85.   1951-60

86.   1961-70

87.   1971-80

88.   1981-90

89.   1991-2000

90.   2001-2010

7.9, 7.9, 9.2, 12.2, 13.0, 13.9, 14.0, 14.0, 18.0, 21.5

WHERE DID THEY COME FROM? – 2

Match the player with the club they joined
Frome Town FC from?

91.   Leigh Burke

92.   Kris Scott

93.   Jon Hayter

94.   Marcus Mapstone

95.   Gary Gardiner

96.   Ollie Knowles (second spell)

97.   Ray Johnston

98.   Paul Elson

99.   Liam Fussell

100.   Connor Roberts

Biggleswade Town, Clevedon Town, Hallen, Mangotsfield United, Melksham Town, Salisbury City, Taunton Town, Tiverton Town, Weston-super-Mare, Yate Town.

WHERE DID THEY GO? - 1

Match the player with the club he left Frome Town to join

101. Damien Preece

102. Dave Allen

103. Kyle Phillips

104. Mark Bartlett

105. Mark Salter (second spell)

106. Kevin Biggs

107. Rod Adams

108. Simon Culliford

109. Bob Perrott

110. Stuart Nethercott

Bitton, Bournemouth & Boscombe Athletic, Clevedon Town, Forest Green Rovers, Gloucester City, Melksham Town, Paulton Rovers, Radstock Town, Shepton Mallet, Welton Rovers.

LEGENDS – 2

Re-arrange the letters to reveal the Frome Town FC legend

111.   NORIEN GRBSIG

112.   ROAAN KEBCARL

113.   TMO MOGES

114.   MAEJI SEECANHEM

115.   MINSO THWIE

116.   REDRAN RINREP

117.   YIRCK HEBTURL

118.   LAUP REDARGIN

119.   TOYN RENDOPU

120.   YELDRAB STEPER

CLUB NICKNAMES – 1

Can you name the Southern League clubs from their nickname?

121. The Field

122. The Generals

123. Kings

124. The Marine

125. The Magpies

126. The Blues

127. The Dragons

128. The Peacocks

129. Tivvy

130. The Dolphins

TOP GOAL SCORERS - 1

*Match the player with the number of goals he scored
for Frome Town*

131.   Dave Allen

132.   Ernie Gibbons

133.   Steve Walkey

134.   Mark Salter

135.   Steve Gay

136.   John McManus

137.   Wyndham Haines

138.   Leslie Taylor

139.   Bill Bush

140.   Marmaduke Date

91, 92, 96, 97, 106, 123, 147, 161, 212, 292.

AWAY DAYS – 2

*If Frome Town would be playing at the following grounds,
which team would they be playing against?*

141. Ladysmead

142. The Viridor Stadium

143. Silver Jubilee Park

144. Tatnam Ground

145. Privett Park

146. The Raymond McEnhill Stadium

147. The Webbswood Stadium

148. Gaywood Park

149. Elmbridge Sports Hub

150. The Meadow

RANDOM SELECTION – 2

151. What colour is Frome Town's home kit?

152. In the 1930s Frome Town goalkeeper George Field attracted scouts from which Football League club?

153. In the 1945/46 season how many players did the Frome Town first team use?

154. The now demolished Covered Terrace which stood for almost fifty years was built in which year?

155. In the mid to late 70s, which former Somerset cricketer made 97 appearances for Frome Town FC?

156. What was the cost of the Frome Town match programme in 1983/84 season?

157. Which Frome Town player had his testimonial on 4 November 1980 against an Southampton XI with him scoring Frome's only goal in a 4-1 defeat?

158. Since their formation, which is Frome Town's most successful decade on average in the League?

159. Who was the 2017/18 Frome Town Women Golden Boot winner with 14 goals?

160. True or false: William G Wright was one of the founder members of Frome Town Football Club?

HAT-TRICK HEROS

Match the player with the hat-trick he scored for Frome Town

161.   vs. Saltash United 3-1 win away on 21 February 1986

162.   vs. Bristol City Colts 5-1 home win on 18 September 1968

163.   vs. Calne Town 3-0 home win on 31 August 1994

164.   vs. Bridport 5-0 home win on 4 December 2004

165.   vs. Westbury United 8-5 home win on 17 November 1945

166.   vs. Wellington 5-1 home win on 27 August 1983

167.   vs. Bridport 4-0 home win on 29 December 1979

168.   vs. Plymouth City 4-1 home win on 3 April 1971

169.   vs. Cinderford Town 5-0 home win on 19 February 1955

170.   vs. Shepton Mallet 5-2 away win on 29 April 1978

Stan Abbott, Charlie Bayliss, Ray Chalk, Phil Curtis, Alan Ford, Steve Gregson, Jimmy Jenkins, Matt Peters, Bryan Wade, Steve Walkey.

TOP APPEARANCES

*Match the player with the appearances he made
for Frome Town*

171.   Steve Gay

172.   Ernie Gibbons

173.   Paul Antell

174.   Roy Bartlett

175.   Dave Allen

176.   Steve Walkey

177.   Mark Salter

178.   Bill Shackleton

179.   Matthew Peters

180.   Mark Bartlett

296, 311, 331, 339, 345, 356, 374, 377, 415, 450.

CLUB NICKNAMES -2

Can you name the Southern League clubs from their nickname?

181.   The Dons

182.   The Row

183.   The Citizens

184.   The Whites

185.   The Foresters

186.   The Kingfishers

187.   The Rams

188.   The Cobblers

189.   The Stags

190.   The Centurions

MULTI-CHOICE AVERAGES

191. How many League matches on average did Frome Town play between 2001 and 2010 – 38, 40, or 42?

192. Between 1931 and 1940 how many goals on average did Frome Town concede in the League – 73, 93 or 103?

193. How many points on average in the League did Frome Town finish with between 2001 and 2010 – 73, 83 or 93?

194. How many League matches on average in a season did Frome Town play between 1904 and 1920 – 10, 15 or 20?

195. How many League matches on average did Frome Town draw between 1981 and 1990 – 7, 9 or 11?

196. How many points on average in the League did Frome Town finish with between 1921 and 1930 – 19, 22 or 25?

197. Between 2001 and 2010 how many on average did Frome Town concede in the League – 38, 42 or 46?

198. How many League matches on average did Frome Town lose between 1991 and 2000 – 14, 18 or 22?

199. How many League matches on average did Frome Town draw between 1904 and 1920 – 2, 5 or 8?

200. How many League matches on average did Frome Town lose between 1904 and 1920 – 5, 7 or 9?

THROUGH THE DECADES – 2

*Can you match the average League goals per season
Frome Town scored with the decade?*

201.   1904-20 (Five seasons less because of World War 1)

202.   1921-30

203.   1931-40

204.   1945-50 (Five seasons less because of World War 2)

205.   1951-60

206.   1961-70

207.   1971-80

208.   1981-90

209.   1991-2000

210.   2001-2010

42.2, 45.0, 48.7, 52.3, 58.2, 73.7, 75.2, 76.7, 80.6, 80.7

POSITIONS PLAYED – 1

Match the player with the position he played at Frome Town FC

211. Rod Adams

212. Alan Crees

213. Ian McLaughlin

214. Derek Viney

215. Steve Gay

216. Alan Powell

217. Paul Lindo

218. Mark Salter

219. Steve Eades

220. Lloyd Chamberlain

Centre-forward, Centre-half, Defender, Full-back, Goalkeeper, Goalkeeper, Left-winger, Midfielder, Striker, Winger.

POSITIONS IN THE LEAGUE – 2

Match the season with the position Frome Town FC finished

221. 2011/12 Southern League Premier Division, 52 points

222. 1978/79 Western League, 75 points

223. 1934/35 Western League Division Two, 45 points

224. 1992/93 Western League Premier Division, 39 points

225. 2002/03 Western League Premier Division, 40 points

226. 1987/88 Western League Premier Division, 30 points

227. 2004/05 Western League Premier Division, 76 points

228. 1999/2000 Western League Division One, 11 points

229. 1926/27 Western League Division Two, 12 points

230. 1965/66 Western League, 37 points

1st, 3rd, 5th, 6th, 8th, 11th, 12th, 15th, 17th, 18th.

SEASON LEAGUE GOALS/APPEARANCES

Match the player with the season he scored the goals/appearances

231.   Roger Coombes 27 goals in 42 appearances

232.   Charlie Thompson 18 goals in 36 appearances

233.   Simon Gale 20 goals in 28 appearances

234.   Pat Talbot 23 goals in 36 appearances

235.   Colin Dredge 18 goals in 37 appearances

236.   Ron Anthony 18 goals in 29 appearances

237.   Ernie Gibbons 27 goals in 34 appearances

238.   Dean Elliott 16 goals in 29 appearances

239.   Phil Curtis 25 goals in 40 appearances

240.   Dave Allen 25 goals in 35 appearances

1907/08, 1924/25, 1936/37, 1949/50, 1963/64, 1968/69, 1974/75, 1983/84, 1992/93, 2003/04.

POSITIONS PLAYED – 2

Match the player with the position he played at Frome Town FC

241.   Tommy Gilbert

242.   Bradley Peters

243.   Kyle Phillips

244.   Phil Purnell

245.   Kenny King

246.   Jamie Cheeseman

247.   Brian Drysdale

248.   Bryan Wade

249.   Damien Preece

250.   Paul Thorpe

Centre-back, Centre-forward, Centre-half, Defender, Full-back, Goalkeeper, Left-back, Midfielder, Striker, Winger.

FROME TOWN WOMEN

251. Which year was Frome Town Women formed?

252. Which League do Frome Town Women play in at the start of the 2018/19 season?

253. Frome Town Women started the 2018/19 season with a 1-0 away win against which club?

254. Which club knocked Frome Town Women out of the SSE Woman's FA Cup 1st qualifying round 5-0 on 2 September 2018?

255. A former Frome Town Women under 14s player Charlotte Buxton signed as a professional in 2018 for which Women's Super League club?

256. Which club did Frome Town Women defeat 4-0 away on 10 March 2019 to win the League title?

257. Which player scored the opening League goal of the 2018/19 season?

258. Who was voted 'Young Player of the Season' for 2017/18?

259. Who was voted 'Player of the Match' in Frome Town Women 9-0 away win at Combe St Nicholas on 15 September 2018?

260. Which position does Enna Christmas play for Frome Town Women?

BROTHERS IN ARMS

Can you match the surname to the brothers whom played for Frome Town

261.   Bradley & Matthew (2000s)

262.   Nigel & Roger (1980s/90s)

263.   Andy & Ian (1990s)

264.   Alan & Paul (1980s)

265.   Alan & John (1960s/70s)

266.   Adam & Matthew (1990s/2000s)

267.   Mike & Nathan (1990s)

268.   Alan & John (1990s)

269.   Ben & Toby (2000s/10s)

270.   Colin & Martin (1970s/80s/90s)

Billing, Dredge, Elson, Ford, Frew, Fricker, Neate, Osman, Peters, Smith.

WYNDHAM HAINES

271.   Which year was Wyndham born – 1900, 1905 or 1910?

272.   Which town was Wyndham born – Frome, Trowbridge or Warminster?

273.   Which position did Wyndham play?

274.   Wyndham scored his last two goals for Frome Town in a 5-2 home defeat on 4 December 1937 against which Wiltshire club?

275.   Which Football League club did Wyndham join from Frome Town in December 1922?

276.   How many first team goals did Wyndham score in his two spells with Frome Town?

277.   Between 1928 and 1932 at which South coast League club did Wyndham make 71 appearances scoring 47 goals?

278.   How many appearances did Wyndham make for the Frome Town first team – 87, 97 or 107?

279.   When Wyndham retired from football he became Landlord of which Frome Pub until 1949?

280.   In 1960 which Football League club did Wyndham become president of the supporters club?

MANAGERS – 1

Match the manager with the time he was in charge at
Frome Town

281.   Derek Brain

282.   Andy Black

283.   Peter Thomas

284.   Phil Morris

285.   Andy Crabtree

286.   Roy Bartlett

287.   Simon Culliford

288.   Doug Hayward

289.   Tommy Edwards

290.   Simon White

1956-57, 1959-67, 1968-70, 1970-78, 1984-86, 1992-94,
1996-98, 2000-02, 2003-05, 2005-09.

TONY POUNDER

291.   Which position did Tony play?

292.   From which club did Tony sign to play for Frome Town in 2000?

293.   How many goals did Tony score for Frome Town between 2000 and 2004?

294.   Which manager signed Tony in 2000 to play for Frome Town?

295.   Which Football League club did Tony make 113 appearances scoring 10 goals from 1990 to 1994?

BRIAN DRYSDALE

296.   From which club did Brian join Frome Town in 1978?

297.   Which League club did Brian gain the honour of the Football League Second Division runners-up in 1975/76?

298.   How many appearances as player/manager did Brian make for Frome Town - 78, 88 or 98?

299.   Which position did Brian play?

300.   Which North-East League club did Brian play making 170 appearances and scoring 2 goals 1965-69?

1978/79

301. How many points did Frome Town finish the season as Western League Premier Champions – 75, 77 or 79?

302. Which manager did Bob Boyd replace in November 1978?

303. Which Frome Town player scored a hat-trick the only one of the Robins entire season, it was on his debut in a 3-0 home win against Barnstaple Town on 11 November 1978?

304. How many first team appearances did both Steve's Gay and Walkey make in all competitions?

305. What was the attendance at Badgers Hill when Frome Town beat Welton Rovers 3-1 on 18 April 1979 – 200, 300 or 400?

306. Frome Town drew how many of their last six League games?

307. Who were Frome Town's first League opponents of the season, a game, which they lost 1-0 at home on 19 August 1978?

308. From 28 October 1978 to 7 May 1979 how many goals did Frome Town concede in all competitions?

309. How many of the 38 League games did Frome Town lose?

310. Which club came runners-up to Frome Town with 74 points?

2001/02

311. Who scored Frome Town's opening League goal of the season at home to Exmouth Town in a 1-1 draw on 18 August 2001?

312. Which two Frome players both made 49 appearances in all competitions?

313. How many matches did Frome Town win from their 38 League games?

314. Which club were runners-up to Frome Town in the League with 84 points?

315. Who was voted Frome Town supporters 'Player of the Year'?

316. Four hat-tricks were scored in this season but how many was in the League?

317. How many goals did Mark Salter score in all competitions – 34, 36 or 38?

318. Which Frome player had a testimonial against Gloucester City in recognition of his 17 years with the club?

319. Which club defeated Frome Town 2-1 in the Les Phillips Cup Final on 12 May 2002 at Twerton Park, Bath?

320. From the above question, what was the attendance for this match – 600, 700 or 800?

MATCH THE YEAR – 1

Match the year with the event which took place.

321. Frome Town are winners of the Western League Alan Young cup.

322. Frome Town are 'Community Club of the Year" (South West).

323. Ernie Gibbons ends the season as Frome Town's top scorer with 9 goals.

324. Paul Thorpe is made Frome Town manager.

325. Mike Butt ends the season with an incredible 52 first team goals in 35 appearances.

326. Home match tickets rises to £12 for an adult to watch Frome Town.

327. Stan Abbott ends the season with an incredible 52 first team goals in 49 appearances.

328. The Frome Town Social Club became "The Venue and Sports Bar".

329. Phil Morris, Geoff Morton-Norris and Alec Castle all step down from their posts within the club.

330. Peace time football kicks-off after World War Two.

1905, 1945, 1955, 1963, 1980, 1994, 2002, 2010, 2012, 2018.

MARK SALTER

331.   Which year was Mark born – 1980, 1982 or 1984?

332.   Which English city was Mark born – Bristol, Coventry or Oxford?

333.   Against which club did Mark make his Frome Town debut on 14 August 1999 in a 3-1 away defeat a game in which he also scored his first goal?

334.   How many appearances did Mark make in his second spell with Frome Town from 2003 to 2006?

335.   Which club did Mark score 32 goals in 25 appearances in all competitions in the 2010/11 season?

336.   Which Football League club signed Mark from Frome Town in October 2002?

337.   From the above question, Mark only scored one Football League goal and this was on 22 March 2003, which club did he score against?

338.   Which position did Mark play?

339.   Which manager signed Mark to Frome Town in 1999?

340.   Mark scored his last Frome Town goal on 10 April 2010 in a 2-1 home win who was the opponents?

PLAYER NICKNAMES - 1

Can you name the Frome Town player from their nickname?

341.   'Bertie'

342.   'Marmy'

343.   'Beppe'

344.   'Maggot'

345.   'Shaker'

346.   'Gigsy'

347.   'Breezer'

348.   'Dusty'

349.   'Percy'

350.   'Salts'

RONNIE BRIGGS

351. From which club did Ronnie join Frome Town in 1968?

352. How international caps did Ronnie win for Northern Ireland?

353. Which position did Ronnie play?

354. How many appearances did Ronnie make for Frome Town – 31, 41 or 51?

355. Ronnie made his international debut for Northern Ireland in April 1962 in a 4-0 defeat to which country?

RAY JOHNSON

356. Who replaced Ray as Goalkeeper in 2006?

357. What was Ray's nickname at Frome Town?

358. In his two spells with Frome Town how many appearances did Ray make - 29, 39 or 49?

359. Which club did Ray join in 2005 sandwiched between his two spells with Frome Town

360. Which Western League Premier Division club was Ray appointed as assistant manager to Terry Moore in 2013/14?

MATCH THE YEAR – 2

Match the year with the event which took place.

361.   Leslie Taylor scores four of the five Frome Town goals away at Chippenham Town.

362.   Bristol Rovers manager Gerry Francis is seen at Badgers Hill.

363.   Dave Allen signs professional forms for Frome Town FC.

364.   "The Boys on the Hill" The Official History of FTFC is published.

365.   The opening takes place of Frome Town dressing rooms.

366.   The old main stand is built at Badgers Hill.

367.   Rod Adams is the first ever Frome Town player to be directly transferred to a League club.

368.   Over 1400 home fans watch Frome Town vs Paulton Rovers in a FA Cup tie.

369.   Giuseppe Sorbara went to Bristol Rovers for a trial.

370.   Former Frome Town player George Bruzas passes away age 89.

1905, 1935, 1948, 1953, 1966, 1974, 1984, 1985, 2002, 2011.

TONY BOOK

371.   Which city was Tony born – Bath, Bristol or Salisbury?

372.   Which position did Tony play?

373.   Which club did Tony join from Frome Town in January 1956?

374.   What was Tony's transfer fee when Joe Mercer signed him to play for Manchester City in 1966?

375.   Which year was Tony inducted into Manchester City's 'Hall of Fame'?

376.   How many appearances did Tony make in his brief spell at Frome Town – 19, 29 or 39?

377.   Which League manager did Tony mostly work with throughout his playing career?

378.   Which League club did Tony first sign for in 1964 for £1,500?

379.   How many goals did Tony score for Frome Town – 3, 13 or 23?

380.   Can you name three of the major honours Tony won with Manchester City from 1968 to 1972?

LEGENDS – 3

Re-arrange the letters to reveal the Frome Town legend

381. NJO THYEAR

382. OBB DYOB

383. ORN KSCID

384. SEVET REGSONG

385. NOJ WOREYCL

386. LANA DRFO

387. MINESO NALLSOI

388. LAUP TENALL

389. KULE BANGILLER

390. WAMTTEH REPETS

MATCH THE YEAR – 3

Match the year with the event which took place

391.   Frome Town are Western League Division Two champions.

392.   Frome Town have one point deducted for fielding an ineligible player.

393.   Frome Town end the season 16th with 58 points in the Southern Premier League.

394.   Richard Coombes scores his very first goal for Frome Town away at Saltash United and it keeps Frome in the Western League Premier Division.

395.   Luke Ballinger with 18 goals is Frome Town's top scorer for the second season in a row.

396.   Frome Town are runners-up in the Western Football League Cup for the first time.

397.   Tim Cuff is top League goal scorer with 11 for Frome Town.

398.   Mark Salter breaks Leslie Taylor's top goal scoring record.

399.   Winchester City defeat Frome Town 2-1 AET in the FA Cup 1st Qualifying Round replay.

400.   Kalem Seconds hits a hat-trick against Taunton Town in a 5-1 home win in the Western League.

1920, 1955, 1964, 1986, 1992, 1999, 2007, 2011, 2016, 2018.

WHERE DID THEY GO? – 2

Match the player with the club he left Frome Town to join

401. John Meggatt

402. Rob Stone

403. Steve Book

404. Stuart Parris

405. Ray Johnson

406. Keith Watkins

407. Ronnie Briggs

408. Dean Griffiths (first spell)

409. Ronnie Dicks

410. Dean Elliot

Brighton & Hove Albion, Chard Town, Glastonbury Town, Gloucester City, Mangotsfield United, Melksham Town, Portishead, Taunton Town, Timsbury Athletic, Welton Rovers.

POSITIONS THEY PLAYED – 3

Match the player with the position he played at Frome Town FC

411.   Pym Bailey

412.   Charlie Bayliss

413.   Tom Pass

414.   Thomas Evans

415.   Mac Miller

416.   Chas Hemmings

417.   Jonathan Davies

418.   Ivor Griffiths

419.   Ashley Caldwell

420.   Alan Lovegrove

Defender, Forward, Full-back, Goalkeeper, Inside-forward, Left-winger, Midfielder, Midfielder, Wing-half, Winger.

PLAYER NICKNAMES – 2

Can you name the Frome Town player from their nickname?

421. 'Jiggy'

422. 'Bubbles'

423. 'Cheeso'

424. 'TJ'

425. 'Sumo'

426. 'Manny'

427. Thorpy'

428. 'Buzz'

429. 'Dimmo'

430. 'Fred'

RANDOM SELECTION – 3

431. Which former Frome Town player with his brother William opened Date Bros shop in the centre of Frome in 1900?

432. What was the admission fee for home games in the seasons of 1979/80 and 1980/81?

433. During 1952 and 1953 what was Frome Town's average home attendance - 500, 750 or 1000?

434. Which minute did Rick Davis score to give Frome Town a 1-0 home win against Kings Langley on 1 September 2018?

435. What was the final score when Frome Town played Paulton Rovers on 1 January 2010 in front of 617 home spectators – 0-0, 1-0 or 0-1?

436. Which club did Mark Salter score against on his 400 appearance for Frome Town in 2009?

437. Which former Arsenal striker did Andy Crabtree sign for Frome Town in 2008?

438. Which late 80s early 90s players father Keith was a professional boxing referee?

439. Which position does Frome Town Women number 10 Charley Ratcliffe play?

440. Which club did Frome Town end up runners-up to in the 2008/09 Western League Premier Division?

PAST OPPONENTS - 1

Fill in the gaps to reveal Frome Town's past opponents

441.   R_D_T_C_

442.   _E_K_H_M

443.   D_V_Z_S

444.   _E_T_U_Y

445.   B_R_S_A_L_

446.   _E_N_H_M

447.   T_V_R_O_

448.   _R_D_E_A_E_

449.   B_I_P_R_

450.   _A_L_S_

PLAYER NICKNAMES – 3

Can you name the Frome Town player from their nickname?

451.   'Bathy' or 'Lord Bath'

452.   'Asho'

453.   'Bang Bang'

454.   'Moose'

455.   'Franksy'

456.   'Barts'

457.   'Dubs'

458.   'Woddy'

459.   'Mets'

460.   'Metal'

PLAYER OF THE SEASON

Can you match the player to the season he won the award?

461.   Connor Roberts

462.   Mike Baker

463.   Andy Dymond

464.   Lee Ashton

465.   Paul Gardiner

466.   Colin Stokes

467.   Jon Crowley

468.   Joe Raynes

469.   Steve Wright

470.   Steve Gay

1966/67, 1974/75, 1976/77, 1981/82, 1983/84, 1992/93, 2001/02, 2006/07, 2016/17, 2017/18.

RANDOM SELECTION – 4

471. Who was voted Frome Town Women' Managers 'Player of the Season' for 2017/18?

472. Which year was Badgers Hill renamed The Aldersmith Stadium?

473. How many players did Frome Town use between 1999 and 2016 – 250, 350 Or 450?

474. How many goals did Bryan Wade score for Frome Town in his 35 appearances from 1993 to 1995 ending up top goal scorer two seasons in a row?

475. On 19 August 1996 Frome Town won 2-1 away to give them their first away win for two years, which club did they defeat?

476. What nationality was the 1950s Frome Town players John McManus and Andy Crawford?

477. Which position did Jack Wyman play – Centre-back, Full-back or Half-back?

478. Which honour did Frome Town manager Andy Black win in 2005?

479. Which Goalkeeper made 68 appearances for Frome Town in the early 1990s?

480. How many different seasons was Mark Salter leading marksman for Frome Town?

PAST OPPONENTS – 2

Fill in the gaps to reveal Frome Town's past opponents

481. _H_R_

482. S_R_E_

483. _A_L_N

484. C_L_E

485. _I_T_N

486. E_M_U_H

487. _O_S_A_

488. M_N_H_A_

489. _A_M_N_T_R

490. T_O_B_I_G_

MANAGERS – 2

Match the manager with the time he was in charge at Frome Town

491.   Gordon Hardy

492.   Adrian Foster

493.   Steve D'Arcy

494.   Josh Jeffries

495.   Darren Perrin

496.   Nick Bunyard

497.   Bill Norman

498.   Steve Ford

499.   Kalem Seconds

500.   Paul Thorpe

1955-56, 1957-58, 1981-84, 1987-89, 1990-91, 2002-03, 2009-13, 2013-15, 2015-16, 2016-18.

TOP GOAL SCORERS – 2

Match the player with the number of goals he scored for Frome Town

501.   Jimmy Clifford

502.   Stan Abbott

503.   Derrick Baber

504.   Alan Ford

505.   Matthew Peters

506.   Phil Curtis

507.   Barrie Simmons

508.   Ray Williams

509.   Colin Dredge

510.   Bill Shackleton

54, 54, 56, 57, 60, 76, 78, 81, 86, 89.

NATIONALITIES

Can you match the Frome Town player with his nationality?

511. Hung Dang

512. Johnny Gorman

513. Eric Laborieux

514. Howard Pritchard

515. Manjit Lallli

516. Giuseppe Sorbara

517. Tom Piotrowski

518. Darren White

519. Sebastian Tylek

520. John McManus

English, French, Irish, Italian, New Zealander, Pakistani, Polish, Scottish, Vietnamese, Welsh.

SEASON TOP GOAL SCORERS

Match the player with the number of seasons he was top goal scorer for Frome Town

521.   Steve Walkey

522.   Mark Salter

523.   Geoff Roost

524.   Steve Gay

525.   Wyndham Haines

526.   Marmaduke Date

527.   Luke Ballinger

528.   Dave Allen

529.   Ernie Gibbons

530.   Leslie Taylor

2, 2, 2, 3, 3, 4, 4, 5, 6, 9.

HOME ATTENDANCES

Match the Frome Town game with the home attendance

531.   Frome Town 1 Weymouth FC 4 played on 16 August 2017

532.   Frome Town 1 Southampton XI 4 played on 4 November 1980

533.   Frome Town 0 Glastonbury Town 0 played on 24 February 1934

534.   Frome Town 0 Hereford FC 3 played on 27 September 2017

535.   Frome Town 3 Weymouth Town 1 played on 6 November 1954

536.   Frome Town 1 Hendon 1 played on 11 August 2018

537.   Frome Town 5 Bristol City Colts 0 played on 26 December 1967

538.   Frome Town 1 Yeovil Town 2 played on 22 July 2017

539.   Frome Town 3 Dorchester Town 1 played on 27 August 1955

540.   Frome Town 0 Northampton Town 4 played on 16 July 2017

245, 305, 408, 474, 531, 613, 1,320, 1,868, 2,500, 4,039.

RANDOM SELECTION – 5

541. What was Andy Crabtree's nickname while at Frome Town FC?

542. Which former Frome Town Women player came out of retirement to sign for the first team on 26 September 2018?

543. Who was Frome Town's first team club captain for the 2018/19 season?

544. Originally installed in 1980, in which year did the new floodlights at a cost of £14,749 each switched on for the home game against Weymouth FC on 16 August?

545. What was Frome Town's average home attendance in the 2013/14 season - 115, 215 or 315?

546. Midfielder George Miller joined Frome Town in January 2016, which two Football League clubs did he have previous experience playing?

547. Who was known as 'Cully' in his time at Frome Town FC?

548. Which club did Frome Town striker Claudio Herbert score four goals against in the Somerset Premier Cup 1st Round at home on 3 October 2012?

549. Which Frome Town player scored a hat-trick in their 5-0 away League win at AFC Totton on 12 November 2013?

550. Which Hertfordshire Football Conference club knocked Frome Town out of the FA Cup 3rd Qualifying Round 1-0 in a replay on 13 October 2014?

BIG WINS

Match the score with the Frome Town fixture

551. Frome Town vs Redditch United played on 14 January 2017

552. Frome Town vs Chippenham Town played on 9 March 1983

553. Frome Town vs Dawlish Town played on 20 March 2004

554. Frome Town vs Paulton Rovers played on 17 November 1962

555. Frome Town vs Minehead played on 20 April 2002

556. Frome Town vs Street played on 1 March 1947

557. Frome Town vs Devizes Town played on 19 August 1965

558. Frome Town vs Shepton Mallet played on 18 January 1936

559. Frome Town vs Peasedown MW played on 26 December 1960

560. Frome Town vs Exmouth Town played on 29 May 1976

6-1, 7-0, 7-0, 7-1, 8-0, 8-1, 9-1, 10-0, 10-1, 11-0.

YEARS AT THE CLUB

Match the player with the time he spent playing
at Frome Town FC

561.   Steve Walkey

562.   Bill Shackleton

563.   Tom Gomes

564.   Roy Bartlett

565.   Matthew Peters

566.   Steve Gay

567.   Sid Carter

568.   Darren Chitty

569.   Aaron Blacker

570.   John Meggatt

1904-20, 1948-58, 1957-70, 1971-79, 1973-85, (1974-80 & 1982-93), 1985-2002, (1994-2003 & 2005), 2002-12, 2009-16.

MATCH THE YEAR – 4

Match the year to the event which took place

571.   Jake Jackson scores a hat-trick in the 3-0 away win at Cambridge City.

572.   Graham Muxworthy signs Dave Smith who was now on his third spell with Frome Town.

573.   Frome Town is only one of nine teams participating in the Wiltshire League.

574.   Club captain Roger Brown is made 'Sportsman of the Year'.

575.   Bill Bailey Groundsman for 40 years at Frome Town FC passes away age 85.

576.   Frome Town Ladies win 3-1 at home in the top of the table clash against Purnell Sports on Sunday 30 September?

577.   Calne & Harris United are beaten 8-1 by Frome Town at the Hill.

578.   Dave Allen leaves first team football to play for the reserves.

579.   With the mortgage paid Frome Town FC finally owns the ground at Badgers Hill.

580.   The new Souvenir shop opens at Frome Town FC.

1908, 1947, 1956, 1962, 1974, 1983, 1987, 1994, 2017, 2018.

RANDOM SELECTION – 6

581. Goalkeeper Darren Behcet signed for Frome Town in 2018 but at which Premier League club academy did he attend?

582. Which season did Captain Richard Crowley won the 'Player of the Year' award?

583. How much was the entrance fee for Frome Town's home League games for the 2018/19 season?

584. Paul Thorpe scored 12 goals for Frome Town but how many appearances did he make in his 4 seasons – 120, 125 or 130?

585. Which Frome Town manager had the best win ratio per games at 65.22%?

586. How many goals did Aaron Blacker score in his 212 appearances for Frome Town?

587. In the first sixteen years of the club's history Frome Town FC only averaged how many draws per season?

588. Which two Football League clubs was Danny Greaves a goalkeeper?

589. Which Midfielder signed for Frome Town from Melksham Town in the summer of 2018?

590. Which position does Johnny Gorman play? He was signed from Northwich Victoria in 2018.

RANDOM SELECTION – 7

591.   Which Frome player received the 'Man of the Match' award for his 2 goals and assist in the 3-0 home win against Walton Casuals on 29 September 2018?

592.   Which Frome player was top goal scorer with 13 in 1977/78?

593.   Which Scottish League club did Frome Town play in a pre-season friendly in 1980?

594.   Which Father and Son played for Frome Town FC in the 1950s/60s and 1980s/90s?

595.   Lewis Powell scored a hat-trick in Frome Town's 4-3 away win at Weston-super-Mare on 6 November 2012, how many of his goals was converted by penalty?

596.   Which Father and Son actually played together in the same Frome Town team in 2002/03 season?

597.   Who was Frome Town's 'Player of the Year' in the 1997/98 season?

598.   In the 2017/18 season how many H&B Tyres 'Man of the Match' awards did Chas Hemmings win?

599.   Which 4 consecutive decades did Tommy Gomes and his son Joe play for Frome Town?

600.   Ricky Hulbert scored a hat-trick in Frome Town's 4-1 home win on 2 November 2011. Who was Frome's opponents?

ANSWERS

CLUB HISTORY
1. 1904
2. The Robins
3. 1919/20
4. Badgers Hill, Frome
5. 2,331 (541 seated)
6. 2012
7. Paulton Rovers
8. Danny Greaves
9. 4-1
10. The Scarlet Runners

CLUB RECORDS
11. (437 starts 13 as substitute = 450)
12. 8th
13. 8,000
14. Boston United
15. True
16. 2012
17. 2011
18. Leslie Taylor
19. Dave Allen
20. Mark Salter

CLUB HONOURS
21. Western League Premier Division Winners
    - 1978/79
22. Wiltshire Football League Premier Division Winners
    - 1909/10
23. Somerset Premier Cup Winners
    - 1966/67
24. Western Football League Cup Winners
    - 1982/83
25. Western League Division Two Runners-up
    - 1954/55
26. Southern Football League Cup Runners-up
    - 2012/13

27. Somerset Senior Cup Winners
    - 1932/33
28. Western League Division One Winners
    - 2001/02
29. Somerset County Football League Premier Division
    - Winners - 1906/07
30. Western Counties Floodlit Cup Winners
    - 1983/84

WHERE DID THEY COME FROM? – 1

31. Tony Pounder	-	Yeovil Town
32. Richard Fey	-	Bristol Manor Farm
33. Steve Book (first spell)	-	Paulton Rovers
34. Paul Randall	-	Glastonbury Town
35. Brian Drysdale	-	Oxford United
36. Phil Purnell	-	Forest Green Rovers
37. Wyndham Haines	-	Weymouth Town
38. Ronnie Briggs	-	Bristol Rovers
39. Mark Salter (second spell)	-	Bath City
40. Bryan Wade	-	Brighton & Hove Albion

LEGENDS – 1

41. Roy Bartlett
42. Leslie Taylor
43. John Meggatt
44. Doug Hayward
45. Dave Allen
46. Rod Adams
47. Steve Walkey
48. Mark Salter
49. Paul Thorpe
50. Steve Gay

POSITIONS IN THE LEAGUE – 1

51. 2017/18 Southern League Premier Division, 61 points - 13th
52. 1975/76 Western League, 61 points - 11th

53. 1983/84 Western League Premier Division, 50 points - 4th
54. 1919/20 Western League Division Two, 22 points - 1st
55. 1989/90 Western League Premier Division, 26 points - 20th
56. 2008/09 Western League Premier Division, 76 points - 2nd
57. 1955/56 Western League Division One, 27 points - 10th
58. 1931/32 Western League Division Two, 37 points - 8th
59. 1998/99 Western League Division One, 26 points - 17th
60. 2005/06 Western League Premier Division, 64 points - 7th

RANDOM SELECTION – 1
61. The Jam
62. Wootton Bassett
63. Titania Hardie
64. 104 x 65m
65. Blue Shirts, Shorts and Socks
66. Black Swan Hotel
67. Roy Bartlett
68. 91
69. 114 goals
70. 102 points

AWAY DAYS – 1
71. Weymouth Town
72. Merthyr Town
73. Basingstoke Town
74. Hartley Witney
75. Farnborough
76. Harrow Borough
77. Dorchester Town
78. Staines Town

79.   Beaconsfield Town
80.   Wimborne Town

THROUGH THE DECADES – 1

81.	1904-20	-	9.2
82.	1921-30	-	7.9
83.	1931-40	-	13.0
84.	1945-50	-	12.2
85.	1951-60	-	13.9
86.	1961-70	-	18.0
87.	1971-80	-	14.0
88.	1981-90	-	14.0
89.	1991-2000	-	7.9
90.	2001-2010	-	21.5

WHERE DID THEY COME FROM? – 2

91.	Leigh Burke	-	Melksham Town
92.	Kris Scott	-	Weston-super-Mare
93.	Jon Hayter	-	Salisbury City
94.	Marcus Mapstone	-	Mangotsfield United
95.	Gary Gardiner	-	Yate Town
96.	Ollie Knowles (second spell)	-	Tiverton Town
97.	Ray Johnston	-	Clevedon Town
98.	Paul Elson	-	Taunton Town
99.	Liam Fussell	-	Hallen
100.	Connor Roberts	-	Biggleswade Town

WHERE DID THEY GO? - 1

101.	Damien Preece	-	Radstock Town
102.	Dave Allen	-	Forest Green Rovers
103.	Kyle Phillips	-	Melksham Town
104.	Mark Bartlett	-	Paulton Rovers
105.	Mark Salter (second spell)	-	Bitton
106.	Kevin Biggs	-	Shepton Mallet
107.	Rod Adams	-	Bournemouth & Boscombe Athletic
108.	Simon Culliford	-	Clevedon Town
109.	Bob Perrot	-	Gloucester City

110.	Stuart Nethercott	-	Welton Rovers

LEGENDS – 2
111. Ronnie Briggs
112. Aaron Blacker
113. Tom Gomes
114. Jamie Cheeseman
115. Simon White
116. Darren Perrin
117. Ricky Hulbert
118. Paul Gardiner
119. Tony Pounder
120. Bradley Peters

CLUB NICKNAMES – 1
121. Mangotsfield Town
122. Chesham United
123. Kings Langley
124. Swindon Supermarine
125. Dorchester Town or Wimborne Town
126. Metropolitan Police FC or Fleet Town
127. Basingstoke Town
128. Taunton Town
129. Tiverton Town
130. Poole Town

TOP GOAL SCORERS - 1
131.	Dave Allen	-	161
132.	Ernie Gibbons	-	123
133.	Steve Walkey	-	106
134.	Mark Salter	-	292
135.	Steve Gay	-	91
136.	John McManus	-	97
137.	Wyndham Haines	-	96
138.	Leslie Taylor	-	212
139.	Bill Bush	-	92
140.	Marmaduke Date	-	147

AWAY DAYS – 2

141. Tiverton Town
142. Taunton Town
143. Hendon
144. Poole Town
145. Gosport Borough
146. Salisbury
147. Swindon Supermarine
148. Kings Langley
149. Walton Casuals
150. Chesham United

RANDOM SELECTION – 2

151. Red Shirts, Red Shorts and Red Socks
152. Reading
153. 58 players used
154. 1953
155. Colin Dredge
156. 15 pence
157. Steve Gay
158. The Noughties (2001-2010)
159. Katie Minty
160. True

HAT-TRICK HEROS

161. vs. Saltash United 3-1 win away on 21 February 1986 - Steve Walkey
162. vs. Bristol City Colts 5-1 home win on 18 September 1968 - Phil Curtis
163. vs. Calne Town 3-0 home win on 31 August 1994 - Bryan Wade
164. vs. Bridport 5-0 home win on 4 December 2004 - Matt Peters
165. vs. Westbury United 8-5 home win on 17 November 1945 - Ray Chalk
166. vs. Wellington 5-1 home win on 27 August 1983 - Jimmy Jenkins

167. vs. Bridport 4-0 home win on 29 December 1979 -
     Steve Gregson
168. vs. Plymouth City 4-1 home win on 3 April 1971 -
     Charlie Bayliss
169. vs. Cinderford Town 5-0 home win on 19 February 1955 -
     Stan Abbott
170. vs. Shepton Mallet 5-2 away win on 29 April 1978 -
     Alan Ford

TOP APPEARANCES
171. Steve Gay   -   415
172. Ernie Gibbons   -   296
173. Paul Antell   -   331
174. Roy Bartlett   -   374
175. Dave Allen   -   377
176. Steve Walkey   -   339
177. Mark Salter   -   450 (437 starts 13 as substitute)
178. Bill Shackleton -   345
179. Matthew Peters   -   311 (291 starts 20 as substitute)
180. Mark Bartlett   -   356

Please note Sid Carter did make 404 joint appearances in the First Team and Reserves combined.

CLUB NICKNAMES – 2
181. Hendon
182. Hartley Witney
183. Winchester City
184. Salisbury
185. Cinderford Town
186. Thatcham Town
187. Beaconsfield Town
188. Street
189. Walton Casuals or AFC Totton
190. Cirencester Town

MULTI-CHOICE AVERAGES
191. 38
192. 93

193.	73
194.	20
195.	11
196.	19
197.	42
198.	22
199.	2
200.	9

THROUGH THE DECADES – 2

201.	1904-20	-	45.0
202.	1921-30	-	48.7
203.	1931-40	-	80.6
204.	1945-50	-	75.2
205.	1951-60	-	73.7
206.	1961-70	-	80.7
207.	1971-80	-	52.3
208.	1981-90	-	58.2
209.	1991-2000	-	42.2
210.	2001-2010	-	76.7

POSITIONS PLAYED – 1

211.	Rod Adams	-	Left-winger
212.	Alan Crees	-	Goalkeeper
213.	Ian McLaughlin	-	Full-back
214.	Derek Viney	-	Centre-forward
215.	Steve Gay	-	Winger
216.	Alan Powell	-	Midfielder
217.	Paul Lindo	-	Defender
218.	Mark Salter	-	Striker
219.	Steve Eades	-	Centre-half
220.	Lloyd Chamberlain	-	Goalkeeper

POSITIONS IN THE LEAGUE – 2

221. 2011/12 Southern League Premier Division, 52 points - 12th

222. 1978/79 Western League, 75 points   - 1st

223.	1934/35 Western League Division Two, 45 points 5th	-
224.	1992/93 Western League Premier Division, 39 points 15th	-
225.	2002/03 Western League Premier Division, 40 points 11th	-
226.	1987/88 Western League Premier Division, 30 points 18th	-
227.	2004/05 Western League Premier Division, 76 points 3rd	-
228.	1999/2000 Western League Division One, 11 points 17th	-
229.	1926/27 Western League Division Two, 12 points 8th	-
230.	1965/66 Western League, 37 points 6th	-

SEASON GOALS/APPEARANCES

231.	Roger Coombes 27 goals in 42 appearances 1963/64	-
232.	Charlie Thompson 18 goals in 36 appearances 1924/25	-
233.	Simon Gale 20 goals in 28 appearances 2003/04	-
234.	Pat Talbot 23 goals in 36 appearances 1949/50	-
235.	Colin Dredge 18 goals in 37 appearances 1983/84	-
236.	Ron Anthony 18 goals in 29 appearances 1936/37	-
237.	Ernie Gibbons 27 goals in 34 appearances 1907/08	-
238.	Dean Elliott 16 goals in 29 appearances 1992/93	-
239.	Phil Curtis 25 goals in 40 appearances 1968/69	-
240.	Dave Allen 25 goals in 35 appearances 1974/75	-

POSITIONS PLAYED – 2

241. Tommy Gilbert   –   Full-back
242. Bradley Peters   Winger
243. Kyle Phillips   –   Goalkeeper
244. Phil Purnell   –   Midfielder
245. Kenny King   –   Defender
246. Jamie Cheeseman   –   Centre-back
247. Brian Drysdale   –   Left-back
248. Bryan Wade   –   Centre-forward
249. Damien Preece   –   Striker
250. Paul Thorpe   –   Centre-half

FROME TOWN WOMEN

251. 1980
252. Somerset County Women's League
253. Bishops Lydeard Reserves
254. Exeter City Women
255. Yeovil Town Ladies
256. Ash Rangers
257. Maya Seviour
258. Emily Petteford
259. Steph Isaacson
260. Forward (Use to play as a Centre-back)

BROTHERS IN ARMS

261. Bradley & Matthew Peters
262. Nigel & Roger Smith
263. Andy & Ian Frew
264. Alan & Paul Elson
265. Alan & John Ford
266. Adam & Matthew Fricker
267. Mike & Nathan Neate
268. Alan & John Billing
269. Ben & Toby Osman
270. Colin & Martin Dredge

WYNDHAM HAINES

271. 1900 (14 July)

272.   Warminster
273.   Centre-forward
274.   Trowbridge Town
275.   Portsmouth
276.   99
277.   Southampton
278.   87
279.   The Vine Tree
280.   Portsmouth

MANAGERS – 1

281.   Derek Brain   -   1970-78 (389 games – win ratio
                                35.73%)
282.   Andy Black   -   2003-05 (79 games – win ratio
                                64.56%)
283.   Peter Thomas   -   1984-86 (69 games – win ratio
                                27.54%)
284.   Phil Morris   -   1992-94 (86 games – win ratio
                                25.58%)
285.   Andy Crabtree -   2005-09 (195 games – win ratio
                                56.41%)
286.   Roy Bartlett   -   1968-70 (88 games – win ratio
                                43.18%)
287.   Simon Culliford-   1996-98 (70 games – win ratio
                                27.14%)
288.   Doug Hayward -   1959-67 (357 games – win ratio
                                45.38%)
289.   Tommy Edwards -   1956-57 (26 games – win ratio
                                26.92%)
290.   Simon White   -   2000-02 (92 games – win ratio
                                65.22%)

TONY POUNDER

291.   Midfielder
292.   Yeovil Town
293.   14
294.   Steve White
295.   Bristol Rovers

BRIAN DRYSDALE

296. Oxford United
297. Bristol City
298. 78
299. Left-back
300. Hartlepool United

1978/79

301. 75 points
302. Derek Brian
303. Steve Gregson
304. 46
305. 400
306. 4
307. Mangotsfield United
308. 11
309. 5
310. Bideford

2001/02

311. Kieron White
312. Bradley Peters and Mark Salter
313. 29
314. Bath City Reserves
315. Lee Ashton
316. One on 20 April 2002 by Mark Salter (Gary Lewis 2) (Giuseppe Sorbara 1)
317. 38
318. Tom Gomes
319. Bideford
320. 700

MATCH THE YEAR – 1

321. 1980
322. 2012
323. 1905
324. 2002
325. 1963

326.   2018
327.   1955
328.   2010
329.   1994
330.   1945

MARK SALTER
331.   1980 (16 March)
332.   Oxford
333.   Ilfracombe Town
334.   311
335.   Bitton
336.   Southend United
337.   Leyton Orient
338.   Forward
339.   Kingsley John
340.   Hungerford Town

PLAYER NICKNAMES - 1
341.   Dave Allen
342.   Marmaduke Date
343.   Giuseppe Sorbara
344.   Matthew Peters
345.   Paul Marsh
346.   Aaron Blacker
347.   Richard Avery
348.   Mark Ford
349.   Phil Purnell
350.   Mark Salter

RONNIE BRIGGS
351.   Bristol Rovers
352.   2
353.   Goalkeeper
354.   41
355.   Wales

RAY JOHNSON
356.   Richard Fey
357   'Razor'
358.   49
359.   Clevedon Town
360.   Odd Down FC

MATCH THE YEAR – 2
361.   1935
362.   1984
363.   1974
364.   2011
365.   1953
366.   1905
367.   1966
368.   1948
369.   2002
370.   1985

TONY BOOK
371.   Bath (4 September 1934)
372.   Right-back
373.   Bath City
374.   £17,000
375.   2004
376.   39
377.   Malcolm Allison
378.   Plymouth Argyle
379.   13
380.   First Division Champions 1968, FA Cup winners 1969,
       Football League Cup winners 1970, European Cup
       Winners Cup 1970, FA Charity Shield 1972.

LEGENDS – 3
381.   Jon Hayter
382.   Bob Boyd
383.   Ron Dicks
384.   Steve Gregson

385.   Jon Crowley
386.   Alan Ford
387.   Simeon Allison
388.   Paul Antell
389.   Luke Ballinger
390.   Matthew Peters

MATCH THE YEAR – 3

391.   1920
392.   1986
393.   2016
394.   1992
395.   2011
396.   1955
397.   1999
398.   2007
399.   2018
400.   1964

WHERE DID THEY GO? – 2

401.   John Meggatt   - Welton Rovers
402.   Rob Stone   - Taunton Town
403.   Steve Book   - Brighton & Hove Albion
404.   Stuart Parris   - Chard Town
405.   Ray Johnson   - Gloucester City
406.   Keith Watkins   - Melksham Town
407.   Ronnie Briggs   - Glastonbury Town
408.   Dean Griffiths (first spell)   - Mangotsfield United
409.   Ronnie Dicks   - Timsbury Athletic
410.   Dean Elliott   - Portishead

POSITIONS THEY PLAYED – 3

411.   Pym Bailey   -   Left-winger
412.   Charlie Bayliss   -   Inside-forward
413.   Tom Pass   -   Goalkeeper
414.   Thomas Evans   -   Defender
415.   Mac Miller   -   Wing-half
416.   Chas Hemmings   -   Midfielder

417.	Jonathan Davies	-	Midfielder
418.	Ivor Griffiths	-	Full-back
419.	Ashley Caldwell	-	Forward
420.	Alan Lovegrove	-	Winger

PLAYER NICKNAMES – 2

421. Jon Hayter
422. Andy Perrett
423. Jamie Cheeseman
424. Rick Davis
425. Simon Hillman
426. Nick Mansfield
427. Paul Thorpe
428. Matthew Walker
429. Karl Diment
430. Chris Butland

RANDOM SELECTION – 3

431. Marmaduke Date
432. 75 pence
433. 1000
434. 86th minute
435. 0-0 draw
436. Bitton
437. Matt Rawlins
438. Grant Evason
439. Right-back
440. Bitton

PAST OPPONENTS - 1

441. Radstock
442. Melksham
443. Devizes
444. Westbury
445. Barnstaple
446. Keynsham
447. Tiverton
448. Bridgewater

449.   Bridport
450.   Dawlish

PLAYER NICKNAMES – 3
451.   Ryan Bath
452.   Lee Ashton
453.   Darren Chitty
454.   Mike Reaney
455.   Andy Franks
456.   Mark Bartlett
457.   Andy Dymond
458.   Steve Walkey
459.   Jack Metcalf
460.   Martin Dredge

PLAYER OF THE SEASON
461.	Connor Roberts	-	2016/17
462.	Mike Baker	-	1966/67
463.	Andy Dymond	-	1983/84
464.	Lee Ashton	-	2001/02
465.	Paul Gardiner	-	1981/82
466.	Colin Stokes	-	1974/75
467.	Jon Crowley	-	2006/07
468.	Joe Raynes	-	2017/18
469.	Steve Wright	-	1992/93
470.	Steve Gay	-	1976/77

RANDOM SELECTION – 4
471.   Keira-Leigh Underhill
472.   2008
473.   350
474.   17 goals
475.   Welton Rovers
476.   Scottish
477.   Half-back
478.   Western League 'Manager of the Year' award
479.   Steve Book
480.   9

PAST OPPONENTS – 2

481. Chard
482. Street
483. Hallen
484. Calne
485. Bitton
486. Exmouth
487. Corsham
488. Minehead
489. Warminster
490. Trowbridge

MANAGERS – 2

491. Gordon Hardy - 1957-58 (70 games – win ratio 32.86%)
492. Adrian Foster   - 2013-15 (87 games – win ratio 31.03%)
493. Steve D'Arcy   - 1981-84 (154 games – win ratio 55.84%)
494. Josh Jeffries   - 2016-18 (87 games – win ratio 42.53%)
495. Darren Perrin   - 2009-13 (191 games – win ratio 42.41%)
496. Nick Bunyard   - 2015-16 (47 games – win ratio 36.17%)
497. Bill Norman   - 1955-56 (49 games – win ratio 32.65%)
498. Steve Ford   - 1990-91 (76 games – win ratio 19.74%)
499. Kalem Seconds - 1987-89 (91 games – win ratio 26.37%)
500. Paul Thorpe   - 2002-03 (61 games – win ratio 34.43%)

TOP GOAL SCORERS - 2

501. Jimmy Clifford   -   78
502. Stan Abbott   -   89
503. Derrick Baber   -   56
504. Alan Ford   -   54
505. Matthew Peters   -   60
506. Phil Curtis   -   86
507. Barrie Simmons   -   57
508. Ray Williams   -   54
509. Colin Dredge   -   81
510. Bill Shackleton   -   76

NATIONALITIES

511. Hung Dang   -   Vietnamese

512.	Johnny Gorman	-	Irish
513.	Eric Laborieux	-	French
514.	Howard Pritchard	-	Welsh
515.	Manjit Lallli	-	Pakistani
516.	Giuseppe Sorbara	-	Italian
517.	Tom Piotrowski	-	English
518.	Darren White	-	New Zealander
519.	Sebastian Tylek	-	Polish
520.	John McManus	-	Scottish

SEASON TOP GOAL SCORERS

521.	Steve Walkey	-	3 - 1983/84, 1985/86, 1986/87.
522.	Mark Salter	-	9 - 1999/2000, 2000/01, 2001/02, 2003/04, 2004/05, 2005/06, 2006/07, 2007/08, 2008/09.
523.	Geoff Roost	-	2 - 1971/72, 1972/73.
524.	Steve Gay	-	2 - 1977/78, 1980/81.
525.	Wyndham Haines	-	4 - 1919/20, 1920/21, 1921/22, 1922/23.
526.	Marmaduke Date	-	3 - 1908/09, 1910/11, 1911/12.
527.	Luke Ballinger	-	2 - 2009/10, 2010/11.
528.	Dave Allen	-	6 - 1974/75, 1975/76, 1979/80, 1982/83, 1984/85, 1988/89.
529.	Ernie Gibbons	-	4 - 1904/05, 1906/07, 1907/08, 1909/10.
530.	Leslie Taylor	-	5 – 1929/30, 1930/31, 1931/32, 1933/34, 1934/35.

HOME ATTENDANCES

531.	Frome Town 1 Weymouth FC 4 played on 16 August 2017 -	408
532.	Frome Town 1 Southampton XI 4 played on 4 November 1980 -	2,500
533.	Frome Town 0 Glastonbury Town 0 played on 24 February 1934 -	1,868
534.	Frome Town 0 Hereford FC 3 played on 27 September 2017 -	531

535. Frome Town 3 Weymouth Town 1 played on 6 November 1954 - 4,039

536. Frome Town 1 Hendon 1 played on 11 August 2018 - 245

537. Frome Town 5 Bristol City Colts 0 played on 26 December 1967 - 613

538. Frome Town 1 Yeovil Town 2 played on 22 July 2017 - 474

539. Frome Town 3 Dorchester Town 1 played on 27 August 1955 - 1,320

540. Frome Town 0 Northampton Town 4 played on 16 July 2017 - 305

RANDOM SELECTION - 5

541. 'Crabby'
542. Lisa Lewer
543. Sam Teale
544. 2017
545. 215
546. Accrington Stanley and Preston North End
547. Simon Culliford
548. Chard Town
549. Ben Wood
550. Boreham Wood FC

BIG WINS

551. Frome Town vs Redditch United played on 14 January 2017 - 8-1

552. Frome Town vs Chippenham Town played on 9 March 1983 - 7-0

553. Frome Town vs Dawlish Town played on 20 March 2004 - 8-0

554. Frome Town vs Paulton Rovers played on 17 November 1962 - 7-1

555. Frome Town vs Minehead played on 20 April 2002 - 7-0

556. Frome Town vs Street played on 1 March 1947 - 10-0

557. Frome Town vs Devizes Town played on 19 August 1965 -   6-1

558. Frome Town vs Shepton Mallet played on 18 January 1936 -   11-0

559. Frome Town vs Peasedown MW played on 26 December 1960 -   10-1

560. Frome Town vs Exmouth Town played on 29 May 1976 -   9-1

YEARS AT THE CLUB

561.	Steve Walkey	-	1974-80 & 1982-93
562.	Bill Shackleton	-	1904-20
563.	Tom Gomes	-	1985-2002
564.	Roy Bartlett	-	1957-70
565.	Matthew Peters	-	2002-12
566.	Steve Gay	-	1973-85
567.	Sid Carter	-	1948-58
568.	Darren Chitty	-	2009-16
569.	Aaron Blacker	-	1994-2003 & 2005
570.	John Meggatt	-	1971-79

MATCH THE YEAR - 4

571. 2017
572. 1987
573. 1908
574. 1974
575. 1956
576. 2018
577. 1962
578. 1994
579. 1947
580. 1983

RANDOM SELECTION - 6

581. West Ham United
582. 1982/83
583. £12
584. 125

585. Simon White
586. 11
587. 2 draws per season the lowest in the entire clubs history
588. Bristol Rovers 2001-04 and Forest Green Rovers 2004-05
589. Chris Allen
590. Winger

RANDOM SELECTION - 7
591. Ryan Bath
592. Steve Gay
593. Dundee FC
594. Roy and Mark Bartlett
595. 2
596. Michael and Lance Spencer
597. Nathan Neate
598. 7
599. Tommy Gomes 1980s/90s and Joe Gomes 2000s/10s
600. Cirencester Town

MEMOIRS OF THE HILL & REVIEWS

"Frome Town was a great experience, to take the team from the bottom of the Southern League South West to the Premier Division on a shoestring budget was certainly a highlight in my managerial career and to see so many Frome supporters at Sholing so happy was amazing.

The supporters were tremendous and people like 'Basher' and so many deserve all the praise going.

Fantastic to see all the hard work put in to this Quiz book and all the credit must go to Kevin in doing so.

And finally, I would like to take this opportunity of wishing Frome Town all the very best in the future and hope their great supporters continue to support the Club."

- Darren Perrin
Manager 2009-2013

"Ever since I can remember all I wanted from playing football for Frome Town Women was to play for the first team and to play on the Frome Town pitch. After playing for the best part of eighteen years for FTWFC I am currently doing that with the added responsibility and the pleasure of being captain.

There is nothing like the emotional rollercoaster that 90 minutes takes you on, as a player, a manager or a spectator. The joys of scoring an important goal, the agony of missing a vital save or the relief of the final whistle to win three points.

Its playing for FTWFC that has enabled me to not only represent my club, my school (where we became National Champions in 2005), but also my county - Somerset. I will be forever thankful for the people that have supported, encouraged and most of all believed in me over the many years I've been playing and continue to do so. Let's hope I have few more seasons left in me"

- Steph Isaacson
2001- Club Captain for two seasons

"A lot of hard work and research has gone in to producing this Quiz book, so great stuff."
- **Geoff Morton-Norris**
Chairman of the Supporters Club

"Frome Town Women is so much more than a football team. It was, is and always will be a family. The pride to play for your town was felt by every player every game, it was an honour to be a part of something that changed opinions of females in football. When we first started to play we had to travel long distances due to lack of teams now there are several local teams, numerous Leagues and competitions it's been a pleasure to watch the acceptance of change. It taught me what you can achieve with commitment and dedication, and to fight for what you believe in even if others were knocking you down. Being part of a team is not something everyone will experience but through it I have gained some amazing friends who I know despite the time apart will always come together and be there for me if I should ever need it. It's not just a game it's family."
- **Lisa Lewer**
1997-2016 & 2018- Captain of the Reserves 2012-16

"I signed for Frome Town from Bristol Manor Farm and was really impressed in the management team of Crabby and Del Boy when we first met. My mate Jon Crowley was Captain and the lads were a different class. I played behind some top players like JC, Laps, Cheeseman and Salter and my biggest highlight was beating Paulton Rovers in the final of the Somerset Cup at Welton that was a great night. We also had an excellent cup run especially almost beating Team Bath but unfortunately lost the replay.
Frome Town is a great club with great people behind the scenes who always have respect for ex-players and always keep in touch. I hope this book brings back many memories and enjoy the test."
- **Richard Fey**
98 appearances 2006-09

"I loved my time playing at Frome Town and it will always be my favourite club that I've ever played for. Also playing with Mark Salter week in week out was always enjoyable. Frome Town is a fantastic club to play for. Enjoy the book."
- **Dean Griffiths**
121(30) appearances, 35 goals 2003-08 & 2016

"I've been at Frome Town for around two seasons now, really enjoy being a part of it, we have some great lads, great management team and the fans really get behind us every game. I can remember settling in very quickly and everyone at the club makes you feel at home. Looking forward to next season. I hope the fans enjoy the book!"
- **Ryan Bath**
Over 75(35) appearances, 13 goals 2017-

"I hope fans will enjoy these 600 testing questions on a range of subjects about this great club."
- **Danny Greaves**
Manager 2018-

"I first played for Frome Town in 1982 a FA Cup tie against Witney Town before signing for Yeovil Town. It was a privilege to play for such a good club, my home team and I've many fond memories and made many friends. Enjoy the test!"
- **Dave Smith**
92 appearances, 18 goals 1982 & 1987-1991

"I have some great memories of my time at Frome Town FC. It's a great club. I was given fantastic support from the fans and from the guys behind the scenes. I was lucky enough to have a brilliant squad of players. We broke many records and I was proud to say in terms of League positions, was the most successful manager thus far."

- Josh Jeffries
Manager 2016-18

"I joined the club a little into the new season and it was the first time I had managed a Premier club on my own. I did however bring with me a qualified Physio in Terry Hardwell, unfortunately he passed away a few years ago. I had to sign a few players whom had not played at that level namely Darren Pool, Mick Pearce, Gary Smith and Richard Coombes, all of these players were important to me and we knew we had to battle to avoid relegation. Away games on the coach were memories where I joined the card school with the lads. I remember when I first let Mick Pearce play, a good left-sided defender, as he came out of the dressing room Sue Merrill commented "Who is that, he can get his hair cut". I remember the well-established players at the club like Steve Walkey, Dave Allen and others made me welcome. Struggling to stay up my son Matthew Southern had to come and play an away game at a top four club.

The last match of the season away to Saltash United we won 1-0 with Richard Coombes scoring the goal and with Welton Rovers drawing 1-1 with Minehead Town we staved off relegation. Though I had kept Frome Town up I still was sacked.

Keep up the good work Kevin you've put a lot of effort into this book."

- John Southern
Manager 1991-92

"I have many fond memories of Frome where I spent most of my playing days as Captain and delighted to be included in this wonderful book and hope you enjoy the read. Memories would include playing alongside the best Centre-half I had the pleasure of playing with in Jamie Cheeseman and of course the renowned Frome striker Mark Salter. This man even had his own beer named after him in the clubhouse, which 'Salter Super Striker' and this was before he had even reached 300 goals for the club! We had many successful seasons and numerous FA Cup runs and good results against higher opposition, quarter final ties in the FA Vase and always scoring when behind in games shooting up the 'hill' to the delight of the loyal clubhouse supporters but one memory that sticks in mind was from the Andy Black era.

After most games at Frome we would go back to Bristol and say goodbye to the local lads with a taunt of 'Let's get back to the big city' and off we would go to find a good pub on route. This is where 'Blacky' would always retrieve a piece of scrunched up paper from his pocket which was handed to him by the old guard who supported us through thick and thin, home and away and always had their own allocated area on the halfway line. Written on this paper was a list of the team for the day and a rating out of 10 including comments, from each supporter, which I am sure to this day would have had some persuasion on Andy's team selection the following week. The same player would receive a zero rating every week, no matter how well they played, followed by a Salter 10 and this soon became a ritual over a beer learning how well we had played that day, or not!"

- Jon Crowley
191(2) appearances, 4 goals 2004-09 and Club Captain for three seasons.

"I have been lucky enough to be part of and remain part of something very special.

I started playing for Frome at the age of ten, I have amazing memories and owe so much to the people who ran, supported and played for Frome Town.

At seventeen I became a coach, courtesy of the club that regularly put players through courses. This was an unforgettable experience that I continued for twelve years. Helping young players enjoy, improve and learn to love the game, their team-mates and the club they played for. I coached not only junior teams but the woman's 1st team as well. Hopefully being a role model to some as I had some great ones in Dawn Prior and Sarah Moxey as I came through the club.

Alongside this I have been treasurer and Chairperson so I have seen first-hand the hard work that is needed throughout the club to run it successfully for the players. I cannot convey the appreciation I have for all the members of Frome Town that help make the club run smoothly.

Frome Town Women hasn't just been a football club for me but a place I know I am safe, can express myself and I can rely upon. It kept me focused on the hardest years as a teenager when it is easy to go off track. It has taught me commitment, passion and loyalty. I have met my closest friends here and made the best of memories. We call it our football family. It is the most special bond between the most diverse of people all pulling together, for each other, for one thing, to put that shirt on and play until you can't play anymore and off the pitch to support each other at any time. Players come and go, but I know the core players would be there in a flash if I needed them.

I am Frome Town Women through and through and I am so thankful to everyone involved, past and present. Each one of you is very special and have made everlasting memories for me. Thank you"

- Alison Bryant
1996- Club Captain for three seasons and Player/Manager for two seasons

"I hope everyone enjoys this book as much as I did. Brings back memories of my debut season at Badgers Hill in 1974/75 as a young twenty-year old and the following two seasons highlighted by the defeat of Yeovil Town by two goals to nil in the FA Cup playing alongside Ray Mabbutt in midfield. I believe this was the last time Yeovil were beaten in an FA Cup qualifying round by a non-League team. These were the days when Frome Town was graced with a few local players such as Dave Allen, Colin Dredge, Steve Walkey and the Ford brothers, John, Alan and Steve."
- Nicholas Peet
90 appearances, 2 goals 1974-78 & 1985-88

"After spells at Southampton FC and Bath City FC I was signed in 2006 as a centre midfielder by Frome Town FC under Manager Andy Crabtree and Derek Graham. I continued to play for the club throughout the following 8 years. Throughout this time Frome Town FC gained two promotions and Somerset Cup success.

During my Frome Town career I had the pleasure of playing alongside many great players who I respect as not only team players but also good friends off the pitch. Under the guidance of Andy Crabtree and Derek Graham we had a successful Western League team including Darren Chitty, Jon Crowley, Jamie Cheeseman, Matt Peters and Mark Salter. This team gained us promotion out of the Western League and secured us the Somerset County Cup. Darren Perrin took charge in the Southern League and two years to the day since winning promotion from the Western League, Frome Town FC beat Sholing 1-0 in the play-off final to secure another promotion into the Southern Premier League. Playing for the team during this time is one of my greatest achievements at Frome Town FC.

Throughout my career I was unfortunate to have been plagued by injuries and had to endure lengthy times out. These included many sprained ankles, medial ligament damage and a fractured tibia. The support I received from the Frome Town FC

management and physio staff was fantastic and helped me to regain fitness on many occasions. Throughout my playing career I built a great rapport with the supporters and still enjoy meeting up with them when watching current games at the club."
- Alex Lapham
228(26) appearances, 19 goals 2006-13

"My memories of Frome Town FC as a player and manager are the happiest of my non-League football career. It's a great club with very welcoming and supportive fans, committee and staff. It's always been a family friendly club and to get where they have on the non-League pyramid with the resources and gate they get is incredible really. I'm happy to have had a small part to play in the club's history and they're my local club so I'll always be a fan. I hope everyone enjoys the book that Kevin has put together and it's nice to be able to contribute."
Nick Bunyard
48(5) appearances, 4 goals 2001-04
Manager 2015-16

"I've been at Frome Town for a couple of months now and to be honest I found it a bit hard to settle in as it was a much higher Division than I was use too but after pre-season and talking to the boys everyone made me feel very welcome. I questioned my ability at first but after getting the confidence with the manager giving me minutes, I scored the winner against Kings Langley and from there the fans, management and team really gave me the belief and thus gained the confidence that I can go on to make a name for myself at Frome Town FC"
- Rick Davis
18(12) appearances, 1 goal 2018 -

"Football is in my blood, inherited from my Dad, who was a Warminster man and played for them to. I was introduced to a football probably around the same time as I learnt to walk, I always wasn't short of anyone to play with either, having two older brothers and another five to follow, my two sisters to, were no doubt dragged in to have a kick around from time to time.

I started my playing career for Frome playing in the reserves initially then two years later I was playing in the first team as a striker who played in the Western League, this was around 1975 until 1979, when an opportunity arose for me to play cricket professionally for Somerset. I returned to play football for the club between 1981 and 1985, during the winter months as you were only contracted between April and September not like now you have a twelve-month contract - my how the game has changed and for the better! At that time Derek Brain was the Manager, we enjoyed success in the cup and League matches beating some good Southern League clubs like Bath City, Poole Town and Yeovil Town.

I was fortunate to play alongside some local lads, like Dave 'Bertie' Allen, Steve Walkey, Nick Peet and Steve Palmer, we all had a great rapport.

The manager's post was replaced by Steve D'Arcy who managed us for three years, we won the Somerset Professional Cup, won the league and were runners up to, so enjoyed a lot of success under his management.

Statistics say I made 208 appearances and scored 81 goals, which I am proud of - there's nothing finer than to play for a club in the town you have been born in!

I enjoy nothing more than watching The Robins home matches when my shifts allow me to. I enjoy chatting to friends and supporters I have known for years and buying a hot drink in the interval - Badgers Hill hasn't changed much at all."

- Colin Dredge
208 appearances, 81 goals 1975-79 & 1981-85

"I joined Frome Town as a 19-year old University of Bath student without knowing any footballing contacts in the South-West. Luckily for me Nick Bunyard took a punt on me and introduced me to some of the best lads I've had the pleasure of sharing a pitch with. When Josh took over the team on and off the pitch went to the next level and was a joy to be part of. The community feel of the club and fans is brilliant, and hopefully now with Danny in charge we can continue to improve on what Nick and Josh had put in place. Good luck with the book"

- Connor Roberts

129(3) appearances, 3 goals 2015-19 And stand in Club Captain

"I am a current Frome Town Women first team player. My journey to reaching this point has been a very long and difficult one. I first joined Frome Town in the under-14 youth section after leaving Purnells. Since then I have achieved great things and developed incredibly as a player and the majority of this is down to Justin Paget. He has helped me to grow in confidence and improve my own ability without him I would not be in this position today.

My fresh start at this new club (Frome) did not go how I had planned it. I missed a tournament and one game due to an injury. Despite this and not being able to play, I was made welcome from the start. Frome won the tournament and Justin said to me "take a medal, your part of this team". From that day I knew this was the right decision for me and I cannot thank Justin and my Frome teammates enough for how welcome and included I felt, as this was a special feeling I had never felt before.

My first game for the club was an evening game which happened to be a friendly against my former club. Before the game I felt apprehensive and nervous about my performance and how my new teammates would get along with me on the pitch. But from the kick-off Justin installed confidence and belief into me and this gave a great result with me scoring a hat-trick and winning the game. The feeling within the team from the girls *was something incredible as it wasn't just a group of players it was a family. When I first started playing for Frome, I was a type of player who was able to play many positions but did not have one specific position I was great at. I started as a right winger then a left winger, then into centre midfield and then I became a striker. Justin worked hard with me to develop my skills and ability in this position and without his guidance I don't know what sort of player I would be now. Throughout my short time so far with the club we have had great success and I am certain this will continue. I have played in cup finals, League cups, League plates and the FA Cup.*

I first signed for the first team at the age of 16 in the 2017-18 football season. This was something I never even thought was possible and was a dream of mine when I first came to the club. Things didn't go to plan in the first season after being relegated from the South West women's football League. Despite this as a team we never gave up and continued to fight. This has led to us remaining unbeaten in the League this season as well as now reaching the Somerset cup final. May long this success continue...UP THE FTWFC!!!"

- Emily Petteford
2014-

"I played most of my games for Frome Town in the Under 18s Floodlight Leagues, I played from the age of fourteen to eighteen, which may well be a record amount of appearances at this level where I played in the position of Centre-midfield. I made my first team debut at the age of nineteen in 2002. I left Frome Town to play for Larkhall Athletic and then Radstock Town where I scored over 100 Western League goals combined. I won the League with Larkhall Athletic. I returned to Frome in 2007 and my greatest memory is playing in the FA Cup against Shepton Mallet on 16 August 2008 a game we won 3-1 at home this match was televised by ITV. I played with some top-quality great lads. After my unfortunate accident in December 2016 Frome Town FC was very supportive to me and my family. I look forward to reading the book when it's published."

- Jamie Mines
11 appearances 2002 & 2007-09

"Being a Local-lad I was always extremely proud to play for Frome Town FC. I probably spent more time on the bench than the pitch, but I still enjoyed every minute of it. Memories such as making my debut in the 6-0 home win against Warminster Town on Boxing Day 2001 or the amazing FA Vase run (in which I actually started a few games) I will never forget and if I hadn't moved away from the area I like to think I would have played plenty more games. I still keep an eye on their results and it's great to see how well they are doing."

- Simon Keates
35(25) appearances, 1 goal 2001-07

"I haven't been playing for Frome Town Women long, but I've had a great experience so far. My best highlight was the Semi-Final against Purnells because it was such a hard but rewarding game and the girls worked amazingly as a team. I'm so thankful that everyone has welcomed me into the club, I really feel like I'm part of the football family and love playing for Frome!"
- *Maisie Harris*
2018-

"My Dad Brian Wilkinson got me in to watching at a young age having played for Frome Town FC himself sadly he passed away in October 2017, but it's now 2019 and some twenty-five years later I still follow them home and away and prefer the buzz, banter and day out with mates and closeness to both management and players, which you do not get in the higher Leagues. Wish you well with the book"
- *Asa Wilkinson*
Life-long Frome Town supporter

"I have very fond memories of my time at Frome Town and playing at Badgers Hill, still remember the cheer coming from the clubhouse and the 'old boys' standing on the halfway line. Being one of Andy Black's first signings it was great being part of an era coinciding with the revival of the team's on field fortunes and having the chance to play alongside some great players. A real highlight was the buzz around the place for the fantastic FA Vase games and the away trips to Skelmersdale United and Jarrow Roofing."
- *Jon McAlinden*
77(3) appearances, 1 goal 2003-06

"I first joined Frome Town Women in the Under-12s that at the time was coached/managed by Lisa Lewer. I was a very nervous and quiet child but throughout the seasons the girls and Lisa helped me grow in confidence; the same team I played with up until the Under-16s, sadly after the season playing as Under-16s the majority of my team were old enough to progress into the adults, where as I was still under sixteen. As I now had no team to play for at Frome I signed for Somerset. After just one season I knew I wasn't where I belonged, and now sixteen, returned to Frome. On my return I signed and played for the reserves. I was managed and coached by Justin Paget and Tim Vine who supported me on my transition from youth to senior football. Through their constant positivity and encouragement, I was prepared to take one step further and play for the first team.

I have now played for the first team for almost five seasons; this one being the most enjoyable one yet. After a tough few seasons our team is going from strength to strength due to Justin and Tim pushing us to play to our full potential and bringing back our team spirit. I am excited to see what's next for FTWFC."

- Keira-Leigh Underhill
2008-

"I played for Frome Town Football Club in the mid-eighties to the early nineties mainly for the reserve team where I played up front with my brother Terry along with club legend Steve Walkey. We won the League thus gaining promotion. I went on to play for the first team along with yet another club legend in Bertie Allen, enjoyable times indeed."

- Trevor Atkinson
10 appearances 1986-91

"I always loved pulling on the Frome Town shirt to play with many good friends Mark Ford, Jon Burr and Darren James to name a few. We were always underdogs and rarely got paid but the atmosphere was great. It was the local lads playing that kept Frome Town at a senior football level, which never went the way of teams like Clandown and others. Never big crowds but the people who watched knew we was giving 100% you can't ask more than that. My early memory of football was when I was approached by a guy named Peter Desisto while playing at a young age for Mells & Vobster, he had money and was going to make Frome Town FC the next big thing, he had some ex-football League players going to play but to be honest I was dubious, but one evening he turned up at my house with Alan Biley an ex-professional with his Rod Stewart haircut. They were both brilliant talkers and I soon signed, they were both really nice guys and great to learn from, Biley scored a few goals but not sure what really happened in the end. They also had an ex-Everton midfielder Gary Stanley sign and play. They tried but it didn't work out as planned. I played under a variety of different managers but the stand out one for me was Mike Leeson, although we lost the majority of our games his organisational skills, attention to detail and most of all his knack of building up your confidence to make you believe in yourself was second to none."

- Steve Ratcliffe
76 appearances, 2 goals 1994-2000 Club Captain for one season

"Despite the constant struggles, financial woes and uncertainty surrounding the club at the time, playing for Frome Town FC was brilliant, the supporters were fanatical and humorous a great club to play for and so many passionate people behind the scenes. Brilliant book Kevin"

- Jon Burr
87 appearances, 20 goals 1994-2000

"I started playing for Frome Town Women when I was ten years old in 2006. Once I've started, I couldn't get enough. I loved playing football and I loved playing for my town. The girls I've met in the club growing up, and that I play with now are always so lovely and it really makes the game so much more enjoyable when you play for a team that works together and wants to win together. I started off playing in the Under-11s and made my way through the age groups, and now I play in the first team squad."
- Nieve Edwards
2006-

"I've been at Frome Town for a little while now, really enjoy being part of the group and made some long-term friendships along the way. Great fans at the club, and Frome Town FC are always producing the youth football which is good and to meet them and have their support on match days. Looking forward too many more seasons and enjoying my football. Hope the fans will enjoy the book!"
- Kris Miller
232(26) appearances, 14 goals 2014-19

"In the early days I use to come up and watch football I was only 5 years old and got the bug. I said to my brother one day "I want to play up here" and he just laughed. Well I did and my first game was on 16 January 1999 away at Pewsey Vale we lost 7-2 and I got 'Man of the Match' this was from the few supporters who came and watched and have been great friends ever since they are Simon Baber, Mark Baber, Steve Jupp, Simon Harding and not forgetting the great Bill Harding and Dave Turner. I played a few years for Frome mainly in the Reserves and have remained at the club ever since, I served on the Committee, been Groundsman and now work in the Clubhouse. My favourite Frome Town player was Goalkeeper Phil Morris. This is a great club and will always be in my heart, I've played with some great players and met some great people on the way."
- Simon Hillman
10 appearances 1998-99

"I joined Frome in the season of 2014-15 as I followed Tim Davis from Weymouth Ladies. Having played against Frome many times, I knew it was a good set up to be joining. I have enjoyed my time here, even though the last couple of seasons have been hard and I think the main reason for that is the younger girls coming into the squad. It's so easy to play with players who are willing to listen and want to improve, and as my days as a player are coming to an end, I'm happy that my last few seasons have been here."
- Karen Perkins
2014-

"Supporters 'Player of the Season' and probably one of my best-ever goals scored against Dawlish Town at home in my first season there was a great memory but every game I played, I loved. Right up to now football has been my life, now a manager last season I still managed to play fourteen games, but recovery is a problem and this season looks like might be the end of a long enjoyable career! If they ever have a Frome Town FC veteran's game' I would love to be a part of it. The people behind the scenes and fans all took to me in my spells at the club."
- **Karl Diment**
65 appearances, 3 goals 1997-99 & 2002-03

"What can I say about Frome Town football club than it was an absolute pleasure to play so many games for them and more than half of them as club captain, I made over 300 appearances scoring lots of goals I played many years with Frome's leading goal scorer Mark Salter but there were so many top players I was proud to play with."
- **Matthew Peters**
311(20) appearances, 60 goals 2002-08 & 2009-12 and Club Captain for three seasons.

"I started playing for Frome Town Women when I was eleven years old, this would have been in 2008. I started off playing up front in the juniors scoring a few goals and then progressed into Right-back, where I play now. Once I turned sixteen, I started playing for the reserves, this was great fun and where I really started to grow my confidence. In January 2015 I got asked to play for the first team for Frome Town Women of course this was a massive jump from anything I had played before and it was a big shock to me. Since then I have played many games in the first team and helped the reserves when needed. I have played with and against some amazing players and have really learnt so much over the past few years. I have also picked up a few injuries

along the way, one being what everyone thought was going to be fatal at the time. In September 2015 we were playing against AEKO Boco in a FA Cup game where I got hit from two metres away with the ball at full force. I went straight down and couldn't get up or move my neck. I was down for about forty minutes on gas and air from the ambulance and had to get taken to hospital luckily, I had just pulled all the muscles in my neck and right shoulder, although not fatal it was very painful! I was out for around 6-8 weeks and although it does still twinge from time to time, I'm still so happy I can play! In March 2016 I was then asked to captain the First Team which I did for a couple of seasons, until around November 2018 which I really did enjoy. I love playing for Frome Town Women and I want to carry on playing for my home town as long as I can. It has really made me the person I am today I have such great team-mates and I love my Sunday's playing. This season has been so successful for us and we have all developed so much. It was great to win the League and Chairman's Cup this season!"
Charley Ratcliffe
2008- Club Captain for two seasons

"Being in my second spell with Frome Town Football Club, I know how good and supportive the people at the club and the town are. I enjoyed playing for the club immensely. I hope everyone enjoys the book"
- Ollie Knowles
52(16) appearances, 3 goals 2015-16 & 2017-19

"I started my time at Frome Town Football Club on 10 April 1992 under the First Team manager Phil Morris, the Reserve team managers was Derek Graham and Darren James. I became Physio, a job I remained in for sixteen years up to 2008 when I became Kit man and still am in this post today. I have made many friends along the way and the club is in my blood, you

could say I have Frome Town embedded through my bones like a piece of Brighton rock. I was honoured with a ten-year service award and this has pride of place in the Supporters Club. Kevin use to be the local bus driver back in 1986 and use to pick my Mum up and drop her off at the football club, all my family were involved in some way or another. Frome Town FC is in a way my life and I hope to remain here for many more years to come."
- Shaun 'Basher' Baker
1992 – 2008 Physio
2008- Kit Man

"My best memory at Frome Town Football Club was scoring on my debut in a 3-1 home win against AFC Hayes on 24 October 2009. I enjoyed many chats after games with Tom Clark. I made some great friends and have many wonderful memories with the club"
- Ben Thomson
129(12) appearances, 17 goals 2009-15

"I remember one match I was on the bench with Assistant Manager Ken Randall he kept the dressing room all together this is where I understood the importance of team spirit. Simon White was one of the best managers I'd played football under in my career. I had the best time of my life at Frome Town FC and enjoyed playing alongside some great players. Very joyful memories indeed."
- Giuseppe Sorbara
17(1) appearances, 11 goals 2001-02

"I never thought that football would have become such a big part of my life. Back in 2008 when I was eleven, I plucked up the courage to join Frome Town Women Under-12s team and haven't looked back since!

I remember playing my first Under-12 League game of junior football. I was incredibly nervous and didn't think I would be any good compared to the others on the team. I played in left midfield and was bricking it! During the game we were awarded a penalty for a bad tackle inside the box and I was chosen to step up and take it. To my amazement the ball crossed the line and everyone supporting us cheered! The final whistle had been blown and we had won the game. Being a rainy Saturday morning, the pitch wasn't in the best of condition, so we took it upon ourselves to celebrate with a few of us sliding on our bellies through the mud. I never thought you could have such a good feeling just from being part of a team or winning a football match. This motivated me to get better and better.

I always played as a Winger during my junior footballing days, I absolutely loved it and continued to grow in confidence every game. As I grew older and progressed through the age rank's I began to understand how to read the game. I recall playing numerous tournaments in the blistering summer heat having ladies coaching us who I now have the pleasure of playing alongside on a regular basis.

When I reached the age of sixteen it was senior football time. I started playing for the reserves and quickly discovered I had become a bit too comfortable playing one position all the time it was a big shock to the system, and I struggled with my confidence massively against bigger and better opposition. I tried to work on building my confidence back up as much as I could but for ages, just couldn't seem to perform well compared to what I had in youth football. I continued to work hard at training and managed to get into the first team, often playing the second half of games until my confidence gradually started coming back. This was made easier after dropping out of the South-West Premier Division after an incredibly difficult season. When Justin and Tim took over as the bosses of the first team and a few of the youngsters that Justin had successfully raised through the footballing ranks came and joined the first team to, the entire team morale changed completely. Everyone's hard work has helped lift everyone's spirits and really helped me with my confidence. Justin even let me loose playing as a Central midfielder, which I now really enjoy! Frome Town Women wouldn't be the same without all the incredible girls that commit themselves to playing for Frome week in, week out. This season we've developed a close bond on and off the pitch which has had a huge impact on the results this season.

I hope to play football for Frome for as long as my body will allow. I also hope that Frome Town Women can continue to grow as a club and be increasingly successful in the future."
Mae Bristow
2008-

"I have great memories of playing for Frome Town on and off between 2000 and 2010. The supporters were excellent and there are too many brilliant team mates to name but the best player I played with was Alex Lapham, he had everything. The best manager was Andy Crabtree – cup finals, promotions and motivational speeches that would have to remain in the dressing room! A couple of favourite games were the 4-3 home win against Truro City and the cup final win against Paulton Rovers. What a great effort with the book."
- Joe Gomes
135(44) appearances, 18 goals 2000-10

"Playing for Frome was always a pleasure for me, being a born and bred Frome boy. I played for the youth team and got my first game for the senior team when I was only sixteen, Steve Ford was manager and we were away to Liskeard Athletic, I was on the bench and we was losing 1-0, Steve put me on (I was a striker back then) with maybe ten minutes left, I remember running down the wing and crossed it along the goal mouth and the

defender scored an own goal ending the game 1-1, so I was chuffed with my debut. I then played for many managers after that. There were good and bad seasons, from when Colin Thurston got thrown in with no budget and only really his Sports House players at his disposal, we still managed to stay up that season. Then we had the great season with Simon White as manager, we had a great bunch of lads with amazing team spirit, we all got on rather well with some great laughs along the way. That was the most successful season for me winning the League and getting to a cup final. Highs and lows but some very good memories."

- Aaron Blacker
212(31) appearances, 11 goals 1994-2003 & 2005

"My Passion for football began at the age of six after going along to my older brother's matches and it wasn't long before I joined and played for Frome Collegians mixed team for five years and then moved to Frome Town Women at the age of eleven to play in the Under-12s girl's-team. As with most young players I played in every position on the pitch but found my preferred position was in defence. It wasn't long before the manager Justin Paget offered me the role of captain which I gladly accepted and skippered the team through to the Under-16s. During this time, I also played in goal at county level for Somerset for two seasons before committing to Frome Town Women aiming to play for the First team. After turning sixteen Justin who had now taken the First team managers role selected me to play Centre-half for the remainder of the 2016-17 season. About half-way through the 2017-18 season I was asked to play in goal which I accepted and have played there ever since. I have really enjoyed my time with Frome Town Women and look forward to seeing how far we can go in the future as we grow in confidence as a team."

- Betty Restorick
2012-

"I hope everyone enjoys this wonderful quiz book about Frome Town Football Club"
- Alex Monks
Over 35(1) appearances 2018 –

"I started at Frome Reserves in the mid-eighties with Kalem Seconds and with Pete Thomas as First Team Manager, and the late Eric Berry as Chairman. I played my first game for the first team at Barry Town a cup match. Sue Merrills was Club Secretary – Auntie Sue as we use to call her (always fussing over something). I also played under Graham Muxworthy, Tony Gough, Lindsay Parsons, John Southern, Kingsley John and Simon White to name a few. Good memories playing alongside Dave 'Bertie' Allen, Steve Walkey, John Goss, Mark Bartlett, Stuart Woodman, Mark Salter, Tony Pounder and Paul Thorpe. So many players over the years with great supporters following us everywhere past and present. I was Player Assistant Manager for the reserves with Mark Bartlett and Lloyd Chamberlain ending in 2010-11 season…happy days."
- Paul Antell
337 appearances, 7 goals 1985-93 & 1996-2001 and Club Captain for two seasons.

"A few memories of my time playing for the Town are from starting out with the Under 18s side to then progressing up through to the first team. A few highlights would be getting promoted from the Western League up into the Southern League, then going on to play in the Premier Division of the Southern League. We were big underdogs the year we went on to win the Somerset Cup. I always loved pulling on the Frome shirt and was very often the only Frome based lad playing for the town, I knew a high percentage of the Frome supporters and my favourite chant from a few select fans was 'Kick um Cowler' to which nine times out of ten I would oblige! Good times."
- Matty Cowler
150(32) appearances, 5 goals 2005-10 & 2014-15 Club Captain for five games in 2014

"From an early age I always loved playing football. I started playing for Frome Town girls in the Under-12s and progressed to play in the Frome Town Women First Team in 2018 this being my first full season. I enjoy the camaraderie and we have a brilliant team spirit, some of us have come through the ranks together so know each other well and this has reflected on to the pitch as we are currently unbeaten in the League and have reached the Somerset Junior Cup Final. I hope to continue playing for many years to come."
- Enna-Marie Christmas
2011-

"I first joined the club at the age of fifteen fighting for a place in the reserve squad. I soon racked up appearances for the reserve team and was soon asked to join up with the first team under Andy Crabtree who was manager at the time. I have to thank Crabby a lot as he looked after me and helped me become a better player with a better understanding of the game. In my first season winning 'Supporters Player' and Under 18s 'Manager' of the season and went on to captain the Somerset County team. After such a good start I struggled to maintain a place in the starting eleven and was in and out finding myself back in the reserves trying to get a call up once again. That call soon came and that season we gained promotion and won the Somerset Premier Cup. My time at Frome was ended that season after struggling with poor results and a change of manager I joined local rivals Radstock Town. I like to thank the Frome Town supporters and the club over the last fifteen years on different occasions I've been back playing. Frome has and is still a big part of my life, for that I thank you. UP THE ROBINS!"
- Jack Metcalf
35(23) appearances 2006-09 & 2015-16

"I have to thank Frome Town for my professional career. I came to Frome from Glastonbury at the age of nineteen, I had been at Glastonbury from thirteen years of age. I just wanted a change and Frome was interested I remember doing pre-season training running around a snowbound pitch. My first game for Frome Town was a pre-season friendly against Bath City on 6 August 1977 where I scored Frome's only goal closely followed by another friendly against Bristol Rovers, where I had a great game and afterwards Colin Dobson came up to me and my Dad and said there was a contract on the table if I wanted to sign for them and to be at Eastville Stadium on Monday morning so I did and the rest is history as they say. I only ever played two games for Frome but very important games for me. Many years later my father Ken helped managed Frome with Simon White. I have a soft spot for Frome and without both Glastonbury and Frome I would never been the player I was, so thank you."
- **Paul Randall**
2 appearances, 1 goal 1977

"I started playing football for Frome Town Women at the age of eleven in the Under 12s progressing to play in the Reserve team, this has helped build up my confidence both in myself and as a player. At the age of seventeen I made my First Team debut where I did get to play about ten minutes spending most of the time on the bench though this was a great experience and one, I hope to repeat in the future. I love playing for Frome Town Women Football Team."
- **Sapphire Fitzgibbon**
2013-

"My time at Frome Town was less than a season, however we managed to get to the Quarter-finals of the FA Vase and a trip to Newcastle. Getting to train at Sunderland's training ground! unfortunately we lost the game, but it was still a great experience. At the time I got to play with some great lads under a good manager in Andy Black. I enjoyed my time there but due to injury and work commitments my time came to an end."
- *Shane Hobbs*
19(2) appearances, 2 goals 2004-05

"I was called by my good friend Tony Pounder. He said that Frome Town wanted to speak to us, I told him I was retiring, but after a long conversation I agreed to pop up and have a word with the manager Simon White and the Chairman Paul McGuinness. Up we went through the country roads and finally got to Frome Town FC. They told us that they wanted to try and change things at the club as they were rock bottom and felt by signing us they would be able to sign better players, so after hearing Simon and Paul promote the club in such a positive way, both Tony and myself signed. Little did I know what an impact signing would have on my life and the friends I would make I did also give them the fantastic news that I was in fact "SUSPENDED" I know a lot of you will gasp with surprise I know but dodgy refereeing had hampered my career for quite a few years by them. The obvious challenge was to turn the culture of losing into winning which isn't easy at any level. Simon told us of the players he wanted to attract to the club and an fantastic amount of talented players joined us and we started to create a bond and got tucked into pre-season. At my age back then I was shocked with the amount of running that the gaffer put us through, but this paid dividends as we started really-well. We pushed hard and many a team made it difficult for us and by the end of the first season we narrowly missed out on promotion, GUTTED I was but from where the club were they were delighted little did the club or fan know that the players got together and we all admitted that we had lost the title and let ourselves down, so we all said that next year we had to work harder so we could win the title again not easy because everyone knew that we were a good team so many time we had to break stubborn defences down. The gaffer again made some good signings and after another very hard pre-season (thanks boss) off we went. This time there was no stopping us good cup run's and tremendous form carried us along and with the fans growing and friendships made this was again the added incentive to win the League. We did it with 2 or 3 games to go and we really partied with the ever-growing fans. The season was capped off with a fine win and a cup final again the Premier League winners Bideford and we took about 500 fans to Bath city's ground but narrowly lost 2-1. After that I was surprised to be asked to be player manager and had a good go at player management but with more experience managers about after 18month I left the club. GUTTED again but understood completely. I was asked again to join the club in later years with Adrian Foster and managed to pick the team up from 2nd bottom to mid-table. Next season was difficult as we always got too many injuries and new that we needed a good start next season which didn't happen to our disappointment. We left the club soon after. I will always cherish my time at Frome and the friends I've made will last forever. I truly thank you all for giving me and my family such a welcome and life experience. Take care everyone it was a true pleasure."

- Paul Thorpe
125(10) appearances, 12 goals 2000-04 and Club Captain for two seasons.
Assistant Manager 2013-16

"I had some great times at FTFC. I remember arriving at the club from Gloucester City and there had been a bit of a change at the club with Darren Perrin coming in. My first game was away at Bracknell and arriving at the ground I did wonder what I'd had let myself in for as the changing rooms were awful, however I scored, and we won so was a nice start. That season was just a *chance for us to get us safe and then the summer few new faces came in and was a remarkable year. The 13-game winning streak was great and the 8-0 victory over North Leigh was also a great memory, however I don't think any fan will disagree the two play-off games were and probably still are the best the club has ever had. The way we started that semi-final was incredible scoring three early goals and blew them out the water to go and win 3-1 with them missing a penalty was a great night. I can remember coming into training on the Saturday before the play-off final on the Bank Holiday Monday and everyone was just excited to get it going. Leaving the ground was great and again I don't think the club has seen anything like it since. Again, we started well and scored early from a great strike from Dean Evans. We then held on and defended for 80 minutes would been helped by the fans who decided to chuck on hundreds of balls onto the pitch at the Sholing keepers end. The whistle went and we had won 1-0 a great journey home was greeted by some great scenes in the club house after. I don't think they will be repeated for a very long time. Some great people behind the scenes at the club and I have all the respect in the world for them and wish them all the very best for the future. I hope the fans continue and some go back to support the club."*

- Luke Ballinger
127 appearances, 43 goals 2009-13

"When I first went to Frome Town Women I was sixteen and just going from a youth League to an adult League playing with people much older than me and I was scared and nervous however from the moment I went to training they took me under their wings and are a lovely bunch of girls. I developed as a person and as a player whilst playing for the team. One of my best memories was in my second season playing for them and in the League we were away to Highnam near Swindon, playing a good game but was down 3-0 at half time, I didn't think there was any way back however the coach and manager gave us a half-time team talk which we needed and we ended up drawing with them 3-3."
- Zoe Porch
2012-

"I played several seasons with both the Reserves and First team in the time I was at Frome and I have never played at a club with the togetherness there was around the place in those years. Both squads had an amazing sense of camaraderie in the dressing rooms, which was clear on the pitch and pushed both teams to be successful, this was also echoed in the club house with everyone being behind both teams all the time. Playing for Frome Town goes down as my favourite footballing years for sure especially winning the cup with both teams. We always had a fantastic following."
- Paul Farrell
101(43) appearances 2005-11

"I started as most parents do with a child playing football for Frome you go to watch and cheer on your daughter. Jodie was an under 10 at the time with Ali Bryant as their manager. Ali was trying to do everything on her own so offered my services, hopefully helping her where I could. That was the start of six seasons of Saturday morning games and Wednesday night training enjoying every single minute of it.

As we moved up through the age groups my youngest Georgia started, so never easy to be two places at once trying to watch both play, I was lucky though as Georgia turn in the under-12s, Jodie was finishing kid's football so got to spend time watching her. The then manager decided to have a break so took over running the team. The next four seasons I was lucky to keep a good squad of players together making many great memories of league wins and loses tournaments entered and won. League cup finals sorry to say both lost!!

The last four seasons has been bringing the young ones on and helping coach with the senior's teams. With the last two running the First team with Tim Vine.

The best thing ever of being a coach/manager is when you see the girls you first coached as a young 12-year old now playing for the first team.

It makes me proud when you stand watching them and how far they have come not only as a player but also as a person.

Hopefully they are still playing for this great club long after I've finally decided to retire.

Frome is a club I will always have a soft spot in my heart for. Many friends made and memories that will last a lifetime."

- Justin Paget
Frome Town Women Manager

"I remember an F.A. cup replay, an evening match at home, 1982/83 season against Witney Town. I think they were in the Southern League. It was a pretty-big game for the town at the time. Ten minutes in I raced through for a pass, a fifty-fifty chance with ex Southampton keeper Ian Turner. I managed to flick the ball by him into the net scoring the first goal. The next thing I knew I was on a stretcher awaiting an ambulance waving the goal celebration to the crowd. After my knee was stitched up at the Victoria hospital, I returned to see Richard Crowley score the winner in a 2-1 win. It was a good season for Frome Town under manager Steve D'Arcy. He had a mix of Bristol players and Frome lads Dave Allen, Colin Dredge, Steve Walkey, Mark Bartlett, Dave Smith and me.

Following my football playing days for the first team I jointly managed the reserves with ex player David Morgan in the late 90s. We only managed half a season even though we were doing quite well. I got too emotionally involved. I remember being sent to the stands by the referee on one occasion in an away game at Easton in Gordano, well actually it was a porta cabin, I kept shouting from the doorway. I think that probably signalled the end of my management career in football."
- **Grant Evason**
52 appearances, 18 goals 1982, 1985, 1988-92, 1994-96 & 1998

"Frome Town Football Club will always be held close to my heart as although my time there was short I was always well supported by not just the club staff and volunteers but by the fans as well, plus the fact both my brothers played there as well, I was always made to feel welcome, as if part of a family."
- **James Billing**
20(10) appearances, 3 goals 2003-04 & 2010-11

"I was at Frome Town FC for about seven to eight years having three different spells playing under six different managers and muking 235 appearances. I started as a seventeen-year old on loan from Bath City in 2005, then re-joined in 2009 under the guidance of Darren Perrin where I went on to have my most successful and enjoyable time in my career winning promotion to the Southern League Premier, this was followed by two seasons under Adrian Foster 2013-15, and one more after that, so on and off my time at Frome Town was from 2005 to 2016. Frome Town will always have a special place in my heart as this is where I spent my best days!"

- Ricky Hulbert
235(53) appearances, 36 goals 2005-06 & 2009-16

"I first joined Frome Town Women when I was ten years old, having previously played for a local mixed team. Football has always been one of my favourite sports, having played it since I was around six years old. I have many fond memories of playing junior football for the club, from winning the League in extra time of a tie-break game to agonising losses. There is nothing quite like the range of emotions you experience on the pitch! Aside from football skills, playing football for the club has given me a real sense of camaraderie and pride in my local team. It was something I always looked forward to on the weekends and still is.

Having played senior football for the past six years, I can definitely-say that this season has been the most rewarding. It has been my first season as a permanent first team player and has given me a lot of confidence after coming back from injury last season. The team have bonded so well together, and it is a joy to be on the pitch with these women every Sunday and to top it off being awarded 'Player's Player of the Season' for 2018/19."

- Laura Didymus
2006-

"I've not been here long but Frome Town is a well-run family club with good ambition for the future. I hope everyone will enjoy this excellent quiz book about the history of Frome Town Football Club."
- *Johnny Gorman*
Over 26(7) appearances, 3 goals 2018-

"It's been an absolute pleasure to have been involved with Frome Town FC for as long as I can remember I have had numerous roles and joined the committee when I turned eighteen in 1988. Since then I have been Match Day Announcer, Match Day Reporter, Club Shop Manager, Turn Style Operator and am currently in charge of the Refreshment Bar and Club Shop along with my sister Sally Lacey. I also head a lengthy time as Bar Manager of the social club. The club has been a big part of my family with my Dad serving many years on the committee and manning the turn style, my Mother was involved with the social club as membership secretary and cleaner for a lot of my youth. The club has a massive part in my heart, and I have the current club badge tattooed on my arm. I have stuck with the club through the hard times and am pleased to see them performing at the standard they do now."
- *Simon Harding*
All round club man of many talents

"It has been a pleasure to have been involved with the club for over 37 years and it has been a large part of the family. I spent a lot of time selling programmes through the years and now currently running the refreshment hut. My Mother and Father was a large part of the club for many years. We have all been there through the good times and bad times."
- *Sally Lacey*
Programme & Refreshment Sales

"On to my memories and time at Badgers Hill or as we called it back in the 80s the temple of science...ha, ha...

I had the pleasure of playing for the town both in the Reserves and First team for around seven years...played with some terrific lads in Walkey, Gomes, Allen, Smith and all the Ford's Dusty, Alan and Steve and of course our Trevor who had the sweetest left peg. Kalem Seconds was the man that got me to come to the Robins shortly after moving from Weston-Super-Mare where I had a couple of seasons. I played in the reserves for the first couple of seasons and say to be honest I think we won the League in my second season but I had a wonderful time at Badgers Hill still today it's the first result I look for on a Saturday. I made my debut under Graham Muxworthy at home on 1 February 1986 against Torrington scoring a header from the edge of the box after Andy Coke crossed from the left the defender totally missed it and I think the ball hit me rather than me head it, but yes went on and won the game 2-0 with Steve Walkey getting the other goal but great memories. I remember Ozzie bringing his Swindon side down pre-season and playing for the Manchester all stars and getting the winner against my own club I wouldn't swap those days for anything I stayed at Frome until I moved off to Spain in 1989. Good luck with the book Kevin"

- Terry Atkinson
20 appearances, 4 goals 1986-89

"When I joined Frome, I realised quickly that they had the potential to do well in the Western League Division 1. At the time we had a great Manager in Simon White and a very good group of players. I felt happy at the Club and was made welcome very quickly and the players, staff and fans created a bond together and in the first season we won the League and got to the Les Phillips Cup Final.

We played some entertaining football with players like Mark Salter, Tony Pounder, Neil Smith and Paul Thorpe to name just a few who made every game enjoyable. The supporters were

great, and I thoroughly enjoyed my time at the Club and even now I look out for their results and hope they continue to be successful."
- Gary Lewis
68(11) appearances, 28 goals 2001-03

"When I started with Frome Town Football Club in 1989 Kalem Seconds was manager, I remember it was a long hard season and we struggled, you could hear the moans from the stands. We eventually finished second from bottom with only Welton Rovers below us. Dave Allen and Steve Walkey two Frome Town legends taught me loads about football I use to play with them as a 16/17 years old on a Sunday for The Crown pub team. I know I can say it was an absolute honour to play for Frome Town Football Club on two separate occasions, even if I wasn't quite good enough"
- Andrew Perrett
51 appearances, 1 goal 1989-90 & 1994-95

"My years I spent at Frome Town were of very fond memories. I very much enjoyed my time there and playing for such a passionate club with passionate supporters. On the home games they use to all stand by the clubhouse house and either support us well if we were winning or give us loads of stick if we were losing but wouldn't change that it was good banter, luckily we had a very good side and use to win a lot more then we lost and in my last season with the club we managed to get promoted which was a nice way to leave the club on.

I am a Bristol lad so use to travel across to Frome 2 to 3 times every week. When I played there, we had a few Bristol lads Richard Fey, Jon Crowley and Gary Powell for a bit to name a few we use to share the driving but again was all good fun.

We had Andy Crabtree (Crabby) as manager and he was a great character very passionate, but in my opinion didn't have much of an idea but as I said before it was lucky he had a good side because we use to get the job done most weeks, I can always remember Derek and Sumo around as well. Derek helping Andy and Basher sorting out the kit etc. All great guys to have around. We had a good team as I said it was mainly built around Jon Crowley and Cheeseman at the back Alex Lapham in midfield and Mark Salter up front. He's a Frome legend as you will know with the amount of games and goals he scored for the club. Great lad as well."

- Adamo Missiato
84(11) 2007-09

"My first memory of Frome Town Football Club was playing against them for Melksham Town in 2003, I have just come out of professional football with Bristol Rovers as an eighteen-year old and didn't know a lot about non-League football. I played Centre-half for Melksham and we lost 5-0 to Frome Town with a certain Mark Salter scoring four of the goals he was one of the best Strikers I've played against. In 2005 I joined Frome Town Football Club they were a good footballing side and had great supporters probably the loudest support in the Western League Toolstation Premier.

Andy Crabtree signed me, and we played three at the back and I enjoyed playing alongside Jon McAlinden and Jon Crowley, we had a fantastic partnership and all the lads gelled instantly. I later went on to form a sole partnership with Crowley, and what a partnership and pleasure it was playing alongside a great defender who could certainly play as well as defend. Frome Town was promoted into the Southern League in 2009, which was a major achievement as we won our last game defeating Dawlish Town 2-1 to get the promotion with Simeon Allison scoring one of the goals of the season. We all certainly noticed the change with the matches getting tougher in the higher league. Darren Perrin then took over as the new manager. We instantly started winning matches. He took the club in a new direction, I called Darren the Jose Mourinho of non-League Football. He bought in new players and added a new professionalism to the club. The first season we finished one point off the play-off places and the following season we hit the play-offs, we then beat Mangotsfield United in the semi-finals and went on to beat Sholing 1-0 in the final to gain promotion to the Southern League Premier Division the highest Frome Town had ever been and I was Club captain at the time, my second promotion and we had overtaken our rivals Paulton Rovers - absolutely fantastic, great times. Two other stand-out players in my eyes was Alex Lapham for his technical ability and Darren Chitty a very good goalie.

As well as the importance of solid defending and keeping clean sheets, I always also found it important to get on the score sheet as often as I could and had a good knack in finding the back of the net often from heading in a corner and often from open play and producing some very good finishing for a central defender. In 2011 I played the first eight games of the season and got injured, seen lots of different Doctors and Physio's and never played again...I was very gutted, I use to travel with the team and attend all the games home and away it was very frustrating. My last game I ever played was away to Oxford City. My overall memories of playing at Frome Town is fantastic ones."

- Jamie Cheeseman

251(2) appearances, 25 goals 2005-11 and Club Captain for three seasons.

"I had some great years at Frome Town FC. We had a great bunch of lads over the years and the squad that Darren Perrin put together was my favourite. We had a great bunch of lads with a tremendous team spirit. It was this team spirit that, against all odds, that made the difference and got us promotion. We had a great 3-1 Semi-final win away against Mangotsfield United in which I saved a penalty. We then went on to win the final a great 1-0 away win where we dug in and ground out the result and we had a great support from the Frome fans who made loads of noise. Frome have always managed to attract a good bunch of lads and good managers. It was a good time in my career and a time I thoroughly enjoyed my time there."
- Darren Chitty
269 appearances 2009-16 and Club Captain for one season.

"I signed for Frome Town 11 September 2015 from Paulton Rovers Nick Bunyard was the manager with Josh Jefferies as his assistant. Later that year I was made the Club captain and have been ever since. I'm currently one of the longest serving players at the club as I've been here for three and a half years, I think Kris Miller is the only player who has been at the club longer. I've made some lifelong friends playing for the club and look forward to making some more over the next few years. Frome Town Football Club have some very passionate supporters, it is a wonderful club to play for and I enjoy every minute on the field"
- Sam Teale
Over 127(6) appearances, 10 goals and Club Captain 2015-
Caretaker Manager 2018

"My first visit to Badgers Hill was a Wiltshire Combination Division One fixture in 1972 when I was playing for the Salisbury team, Old Manor. The next time I played there was in a couple of Frome Sunday League finals for Chapmanslade in the early nineties. It was during this time that I was in charge of the Frome

Sunday League select team and we played our home fixtures at Badgers Hill and was fortunate to win the Mavis Cup with the team that included some great players from the town, Bertie Allen, Steve Walkey, Mark Ford and goalkeeper Roger Smith. I was now forty-five when I got a call from Frome Town to play for the reserves, because Mark Jones had stopped playing and left them without a goalkeeper. Now Chairman of the Supporters Club Geoff Morton-Norris was the Chairman of the football club at-this-time. I was fortunate to play alongside some legends in that side Bertie Allen and Steve Walkey who was the Manager, Dave and Matthew Walker (father and son), Colin Dredge, Dave Morgan, Nicky Peet, Andy Franks, Ken Airey and Darren James also number one Kit Man Shaun Baker joined us as a sixteen-year old and has been ever present at the club since. During this period there were two young boys who would stand behind my goal, always supporting me, who both went on to play important roles in the future of Frome Town football club, Ian Pearce, who later became our Secretary for many years before he left to live in Aberdare, Wales and the other Gavin Ayres who was the Chairman when we had such a successful run in the Western Premier League and then got promotion to the Southern League. In 2005 I joined Tom Saunders as his number two at Odd Down for a season, it was mid-season and Andy Crabtree who played for me at Amesbury and was my assistant at Warminster Town for a season previously was given the job as Manager of Frome Town, and asked me to join him as his assistant, I asked him to wait until the following season as I wanted to finish the year at Odd Down, which he agreed to.

Then began a great journey with Andy, a few hic-cups on the way, finishing 3rd, 4th, and in 2008/09 we finished runners-up in the Western League getting promoted to the Southern League and-also winning the Somerset Premier Cup beating Paulton Rovers in the final, unfortunately after a dismal start the new Committee decided to let Andy go, and replace him with my old boss Darren Perrin. The club then climbed even further up the pyramid getting promoted to the Southern Premier League, unfortunately Darren was asked to leave at the end of March 2013, with the club looking destined for relegation with nine games to go. I was given the task to finish off the season, so I persuaded County Coach & UEFA A license Mick Byrne to be my number two and we finished in style, winning three, drawing four and losing only two, we finished out of the bottom four.

The following season I was persuaded to take the manager's job on permanently against my better judgement, and after only getting eight points from the first nine games I was sacked although not in the bottom four at this time. My squad was ravaged by injuries especially in mid-field. It was a decent young squad to be fair, which included Darren Chitty, Jon Crowley, Matthew Cowler, Alex Lapham and Jack Metcalf. In 2015 I was approached to return to my beloved Frome Town by Nick Bunyard who had turned the club around in a short period of time, but never really got to work with Nick as Josh Jefferies took over and I ended up helping him in a small way, when we had our most successful period in the Southern Premier League for two seasons unfortunately after a bad run after the New Year and having family problems Josh understandingly called it a day and Ben Cleverley his number two felt it was his duty to accompany him. This left Club Captain Sam Teale and I to finish the season off in charge, and as a number of players also left and it was transfer deadline, we had a difficult time going down to Gosport with ten me, including heroic Marcus Mapstone, on one leg and a youth team player. Ollie Knight and Ollie Knowles travelled separately to this game from London and Tiverton even though they knew we only had nine fit men and made me realise what a good bunch of lads we had at the club. We managed to draw one game and finish off the season with a win. This period showed how those ten players really cared about Frome Town football club.

Then we have a new era, with a really dedicated and talented manager in Danny Greaves."

- Derek Graham
Caretaker Manager 2012-13
Manager 2013-14
And assistant to many Managers

"Playing for Frome was some of my best memories from football. I played with some very talented players and won many games. My best memories would be a good run in the FA Cup where we were eventually knocked out in a replay by Salisbury City. The other stand out memory would be the FA Vase run to the Quarter finals however I always wonder how far we could of went without the injuries and suspensions we had against Jarrow Roofing. Best of luck with the book."

- Dean Ranger
148(16) appearances, 2 goals 2004-08 and Club Captain for one season

"It was an honour to have played for Frome Town after Joining from Welton Rovers in 1997, I have to be thankful to Simon Culliford for given me a chance at first team football.
I will always remember the game against Cinderford Town at home in the FA Cup preliminary round on 21 August 1999 where I had to mark my Trowbridge Town favourite Adrian Harris, who I had watched for many years before. He must of been about 40 years old, a great player but a difficult player to play against, we lost the game 4-0.
Frome Town is always a club I follow and one that I am proud to say I played for."

- Paul Bendell
47 appearances, 13 goals 1997-2000

"I had some amazing memories at Frome Town football club, I scored my first goal on the 7 October 2006 in a 3-1 away win at Poole Town in the FA Vase and as I remember was one of seven players who made over forty appearances this season and ended it scoring seven goals. They are one of the most-friendliest clubs I've ever played for and always a great bunch of lads and management team. The fans were always on our side whether we won or lost."

- Sam Duggan
110(25) appearances, 20 goals 2006-09

"I had only had one season at Frome Town football club but it was a good one, I felt like Josh Jeffries gave me a great opportunity bringing me to the club and in the end I think I played every game apart from one with a great bunch of players. It was an enjoyable season for me scoring 12 goals from midfield and being awarded 'Player of the Year' in my time at the club."

- Joe Raynes
49(1) appearances, 12 goals 2017-18

"I came into the club just over six years ago as the Manager of the reserves. I had four great years as the manager and the last two years I was asked if I would like to help with the First team as Assistant Manager and as the reserves was not running for the season, I could not turn it down.

This season I was asked to be the Chairman of Frome Town Women and I think it is a great honour. Every year with the Frome Town Women, it has got better and better and to top it all to win the League with a game to spare, absolutely fantastic."

- Tim Vine
Frome Town Women Chairman & Assistant Manager

"This is my first full season and it's a great pleasure to pull on the Frome Town Women shirt every Sunday and be part of the team, they are a great bunch of ladies and to win the League this season with a game to go was fantastic and also to win the Chairman's Cup and scoring a hat-trick in our victory"
- Maya Seviour
2015-

"Frome Town Women are a pleasure to play for, we have a brilliant team spirit which has shown throughout this season on the field with us winning the League and the Chairman's Cup and getting to the Somerset Junior Cup final. Being awarded 'Young Player of the Season' for 2018/19 is a personal highlight in my playing career."
- Mary Brant
2015-

Appendix 1

Other Notable Players

Bill Shackleton	345 appearances, 76 goals 1904-14 & 1919-21
Ernie Gibbons	296 appearances, 123 goals 1904-14 & 1919-21
Dinkie Doel	120 appearances 1946-49
Sid Carter	404 combined appearances, 9 goals 1948-58
John McManus	212 combined appearances, 110 goals 1953-59
Roy Bartlett	296 appearances, 50 goals 1960-69
Mike Chedgy	276 appearances, 6 goals 1964-71
Barrie Simmons	162 appearances, 57 goals 1964-69
Ron Curtis	169 appearances, 10 goals 1966-67 & 1969-73
John Ford	163 appearances 1966-74
Alan Ford	171 appearances, 54 goals 1966-67 & 1972-79
David Gray	282 appearances, 16 goals 1971-79
John Meggatt	293 appearances, 18 goals 1971-79
Steve Walkey	339 appearances, 106 goals 1974-80 & 1982-93

Steve Gay	415 appearances, 91 goals 1973-85
David Allen	377 appearances, 161 goals 1974-76, 1979-81, 1982-86, 1988-90 & 1991-96
Ron Dicks	154 appearances, 1 goal 1977-81
Phil Morris	133 appearances 1978-81
Paul Gardiner	245 appearances, 15 goals 1978-84
Mark Bartlett	356 appearances, 28 goals 1981-83, 1985-92 & 1996-98
John Billing	61 appearances, 11 goals 1991-92 & 1994-96
Alan Billing	72 appearances, 1 goal 1994-97
Tony Pounder	129(2) appearances, 14 goals 2000-04
Neil Smith	127(18) appearances, 7 goals 2000-04
Stuart Parris	99 appearances, 1 goal 2000-04
Matthew Fricker	81(6) appearances, 33 goals 2000-04
Bradley Peters	124(4) appearances, 29 goals 2001-03 & 2004-06
Richard Lindegaard	130(14) appearances, 2 goals 2002-06
Damien Preece	133(61) appearances, 17 goals 2002-07
Simon Gale	47(11) appearances, 22 goals 2003-05
Sam Jarman	103(27) appearances, 9 goals 2003-06
Jon Hayter	95(6) appearances, 33 goals 2003-06
Simeon Allison	214(28) appearances, 37 goals 2005-11

Appendix 2

FROME TOWN FOOTBALL CLUB - PLAYING RECORD

LEAGUE RECORDS

	P	W	D	L	F	A
Southern League Premier	310	101	85	124	405	494 (up to 2017/18)
Southern League Division 1 South & West	82	44	22	16	145	75
Western League Premier	1536	595	352	589	2395	2427
Western League Division One	385	124	54	207	625	888
Western League Division Two	665	288	110	267	1590	1567
Somerset Senior League	126	53	17	11	280	270
Wiltshire League	304	154	40	110	773	632
Wiltshire League Division One	256	93	37	126	578	681
Bristol Suburban League	24	11	4	9	71	59
Bristol Charity League	10	2	4	4	16	31
Midsomer Norton Charity League	18	6	3	9	20	21
TOTAL	**3716**	**1471**	**728**	**1472**	**6898**	**7145**

CUP RECORDS

	P	W	D	L	F	A	
FA Cup	174	63	38	73	238	306	(up to 2018/19)
FA Trophy	56	15	10	31	67	93	(up to 2018/19)
FA Vase	41	18	4	19	65	64	
Southern League Cup	21	10	4	7	29	32	(up to 2018/19)
TOTAL	**292**	**106**	**56**	**130**	**399**	**495**	

OVERALL

	P	W	D	L	F	A
Leagues	3716	1471	728	1472	6898	7145
Cups	292	106	56	130	399	495
TOTAL	**4008**	**1577**	**784**	**1602**	**7297**	**7640**

The above information supplied by Ian Pearce

Appendix 3

Frome Town AFC Manager Statistics
Complete record of individual managers in competitive fixtures.
The team was run by the committee from its formation in 1904
through to 1953

** From, To, Name, First Game in Charge, P W D L F A, Reason for
Leaving*

* 1953/54-1953/54 Ray Wright 22/08/53 - Chippenham Res 1
FTFC 0 (West Div 2) - 24 13 4 7 56 46 Resigned
* 1953/54-1954/55 Jock Wilson Fairweathers 13/02/54 - FTFC 8
Stonehouse Res (West Div 2) - 66 42 12 13 192 84 Resigned
* 1955/56-1955/56 Bill Norman 20/08/55 - Barnstaple 2 FTFC 1
(Western Div 1) - 49 16 13 20 105 98 Resigned
* 1956/57-1956/57 Tommy Edwards 18/08/56 - Barnstaple 9 FTFC
1 (Western Div 1) - 26 7 2 17 35 72 Sacked
* 1956/57-1956/57 Ran by Committee (Caretaker) 09/02/57 -
FTFC 1 Taunton 2 (Western Div 1) - 3 0 0 3 3 9
* 1956/57-1958/59 Gordon Hardy 02/03/57 - FTFC 0 Salisbury 2
(Western Div 1) - 70 23 9 38 115 168 Resigned
* 1958/59-1958/59 Ran by Committee (Caretaker) 06/12/58 -
Weymouth Res 7 FTFC 0 (West Div 1) - 5 0 1 4 4 21
* 1958/59-1966/67 Doug Hayward 03/01/59 - Poole Town Res 5
FTFC 2 (West Div 1) - 357 162 62 133 767 663 Resigned
* 1967/68-1967/68 John Doughty & Roy Bartlett 19/08/67 -
Salisbury 3 FTFC 0 (Western League) - 45 24 7 14 106 81 Doughty
joined Radstock
* 1968/69-1969/70 Roy Bartlett 17/08/68 - FTFC 1 Devizes 1
(Western League) - 88 38 22 28 141 130 Resigned
* 1970/71-1978/79 Derek Brain 15/08/70 - Bridport 0 FTFC 2
(Western League) - 389 139 97 153 569 608 Resigned
* 1978/79-1978/79 Bob Boyd 18/11/78 - Glastonbury 0 FTFC 3
(Western Prem) - 29 18 9 2 43 11 Resigned (Bath City)
* 1979/80-1979/80 Bryan Drysdale 18/08/79 - Weston-s-Mare 2
FTFC 1 (Western Prem) - 53 28 13 12 94 53 Sacked
* 1980/81-1981/82 Bob Boyd 16/08/80 - FTFC 5 Mangotsfield 0
(Western Prem) - 66 28 11 27 109 100 Resigned

* 1981/82-1981/82 Mike Malpas (Caretaker) 24/10/81 - FTFC 3 Wellington 2 (Western Prem) - 2 2 0 0 5 3
* 1981/82-1983/84 Steve D'Arcy 07/11/81 - FTFC 8 Bridgwater 1 (Western Prem) - 154 86 42 26 302 145 Resigned
* 1984/85-1985/86 Peter Thomas 18/08/84 - Minehead 3 FTFC 4 (Western Prem) - 69 19 21 29 89 103 Sacked
* 1985/86-1985/86 Kalem Seconds & Roy Bartlett (Caretaker) 01/02/86 - FTFC 2 Torrington 0 (Western Prem) - 21 7 5 9 26 35
* 1986/87-1987/88 Graham Muxworthy 16/08/86 - Plymouth Res 0 FTFC 2 (Western Prem) - 62 15 16 31 68 100 Sacked
* 1987/88-1989/90 Kalem Seconds 13/10/87 - Clevedon Town 0 FTFC 2 (Western Prem) - 91 24 23 44 108 172 Sacked
* 1989/90-1989/90 Steve Coles 09/09/89 - Bideford 0 FTFC 0 (Western Prem) - 15 1 4 10 13 30 Resigned
* 1989/90-1989/90 Lindsay Parsons 04/11/89 - FTFC 1 Saltash Utd (Western Prem) - 50 11 12 27 65 95 Resigned
* 1990/91-1991/92 Steve Ford 24/11/90 - FTFC 2 Ottery St Mary 1 (Western Prem) - 36 12 5 18 38 73 Resigned
* 1991/92-1991/92 John Southern 02/10/91 - FTFC 1 Clevedon 2 (Western Prem) - 35 8 5 22 39 75 Sacked
* 1992/93-1993/94 Phil Morris 15/08/92 - FTFC 1 Exmouth 4 (Western Prem) - 86 22 20 44 104 163 Resigned
* 1994/95-1994/95 Steve Ford 20/08/94 - Barnstaple 1 FTFC 0 (Western Prem) - 40 3 5 32 43 117 Resigned
* 1995/96-1996/97 Mike Leeson 19/08/95 - FTFC 4 Barnstaple 1 (Western Prem) - 57 11 12 34 57 132 Sacked
* 1996/97-1997/98 Simon Culliford 02/11/96 - Warminster 0 FTFC 1 (Western Div 1) - 70 19 14 37 91 140 Resigned
* 1998/99-1998/99 Colin Thurston 15/08/98 - FTFC 1 Pewsey Vale 0 (Western Div 1) - 37 6 5 26 40 108 Sacked Paul Antell & Keith Ball (Caretaker) 17/04/99 - Corsham 0 FTFC 3 (Western Div 1) - 3 1 0 2 7 9
* 1999/00-1999/00 Kingsley John 14/08/99 - Ilfracombe 3 FTFC 1 (Western Div 1) - 13 2 0 11 15 37 Sacked Keith Ball & Ali Belcher 16/10/99 - FTFC 2 Calne 2 (Western Div 1) - 26 3 2 21 26 70 Sacked
* 2000/01-2001/02 Simon White 12/08/00 - FTFC 3 Corsham 1 (Western Div 1) - 92 60 9 23 218 99 Sacked - Off Field Issues

* 2002/03-2003/04 Paul Thorpe 17/08/02 - Elmore 1 FTFC 2 (Western Prem) - 61 21 11 29 99 115 Mutual Consent
* 2003/04 " Andrew Crabtree (Caretaker) 29/11/03 - Melksham 1 FTFC 3 (Western Prem) - 1 1 0 0 3 1
* 2005/06 Andy Black 13/12/03 - Bridgwater 0 FTFC 1 (Western Prem) - 79 51 13 15 175 83 Sacked - FAC Withdrawl
* 2005/06-2005/06 Andrew Crabtree (Caretaker) 03/09/05 - Keynsham 0 FTFC 4 (Western Prem) - 7 3 2 2 10 7
* 2005/06-2009/10 Andrew Crabtree 01/10/05 - FTFC 2 Corsham 1 (Western Prem) - 195 110 35 50 368 225 Sacked - Results
* 2009/10-2012/13 Darren Perrin 19/09/09 - FTFC 2 North Leigh 1 (South Div One) - 191 81 52 58 284 218 Sacked - Results
* 2012/13-2012/13 Derek Graham (Caretaker) 30/03/13 - FTFC 3 Kettering Town 1 (Southern Prem) - 7 3 2 2 9 6
* 2012/13-2013/14 Derek Graham 24/04/13 - FTFC 1 Gosport Boro 1 (Southern Prem) - 13 2 5 6 9 22 Sacked - Results
* 2013/14-2013/14 Lloyd Chamberlain (Caretaker) 01/10/13 - Street 1 FTFC 3 (Somerset Prem Cup) - 4 2 1 1 10 8
* 2013/14-2013/14 Brian O'Donnell 16/10/13 - FTFC 1 Poole Town 1 (FA Trophy) - 12 3 3 6 17 26 Sacked - Results
* 2013/14-2015/16 Adrian Foster 26/12/13 - Chippenham 3 FTFC 3 (Southern Prem) - 87 27 21 42 113 147 Sacked - Results
* 2015/16-2015/16 Lloyd Chamberlain (Caretaker) 29/08/15 - FTFC 1 Kettering Town 2 (Southern Prem) - 3 0 0 3 1 11
* 2015/16-2015/16 Nick Bunyard 09/09/15 - FTFC 1 Larkhall Ath 1 (Southern Lge Cup) - 47 17 16 14 59 61 Suspended by FA
* 2016/17-2017-18 Josh Jefferies 06/08/16 - FTFC 2 Hayes & Yeading 1 (Southern Prem) - 87 37 20 30 153 148 Resigned
* 2017/18-2017/18 Sam Teale (Caretaker) 07/04/18 - Hitchin Town 5 FTFC 1 (Southern Prem) - 5 1 1 3 5 15
* 2018-19 Danny Greaves 11/08/18 – FTFC 1 Hendon 1 (Southern Prem)

* The above information supplied by Ian Pearce

ABOUT THE AUTHOR

Kevin Snelgrove was born in Frome, Somerset, in 1960.

A prolific author, Kevin has written over 80 books on a range of subjects, including football, sports, television, music, health and leisure. Many of his books have been endorsed by celebrities and sports personalities such as Richard Wilson, Nicholas Parsons, Fenella Fielding, Ian Holloway and Neil Warnock.

Kevin has also recently taken up acting and was involved in the 2012 film The Seasoning House with Sean Pertwee and Rosie Day. During his career, Kevin has appeared in TV, radio, DVD and in numerous newspapers and magazines.

Having worked with people with Autistic Spectrum Disorder (ASD) for 35 years, in 2013 Kevin decided to use his experience to benefit others and wrote a book about the subject.

Kevin lives in Frome with his wife Julie. He has four children; Samantha, Kate, Charlotte and Samuel, a grandson Reuben and granddaughter Millie.

www.apexpublishing.co.uk